My Spiritual
Journey

Night Club Manager, Orphanage Worker,
Psychologist

Genevieve,

a great year at
AC, you truched
a lot of lifes.

Jeff

Jeff Baird, Ph.D.

ISBN 978-1-64140-583-6 (paperback)
ISBN 978-1-64140-584-3 (digital)

Christian Faith Publishing, Inc.
832 Park Avenue
Meadville, PA 16335
www.christianfaithpublishing.com

Printed in the United States of America

Dedicated with all my love
to my fantastic wife, Monica.
I came across the ocean to work with the children of Romania,
and what a blessing it was when I found you.

CONTENTS

ACKNOWLEDGEMENTS

I am deeply grateful to Dr. Sabrina (Brina) Rood for helping me get my book off the ground with your many talents of typing, editing and direction. Brina, your encouragement, humor and support was truly a blessing.

To Stefania Alexandru and Anil Sharma. Thank you Stefi for your knowledge on the steps of transforming my notebook of writing to a book. Thank you Anil for your assistance on the photography side. Helping download my pictures to the publisher taking various photos and patience with me trying to navigate the computer was deeply appreciated.

Special thanks to Kimberly Schwandt and Amanda Beary from Christian Faith Publishing. Kimberly, walking me through the beginning stages of publishing was very helpful. Amanda, your editing expertise and advice made for a better book.

INTRODUCTION

When you really think about it, everyone has a story to tell, an interesting life journey. I have been asked, "Why don't you write a book about your experiences?" Like most major undertakings, I have spent time in reflection and prayer on this matter. I believe this is what God wants me to do.

I'm not an expert on any specific topic like so many writers. I don't even consider myself a writer but more of a storyteller. Hopefully, reading this book will stir up memories in your own life. Pull out the photos, letters, and yearbooks; do this with your family members. We all have meaningful histories and stories to share. Looking at our memories will bring up some joyful times and also some difficult times. Wonderful and painful memories shape who we are.

Behind some of my most satisfying accomplishments, there has always been adversity. It makes the outcome even sweeter. What happens when you can't get things back to normal, no matter how hard you try? People will try to create a new normal when a tragedy strikes. This is a never-ending battle of will, especially when a loved one dies suddenly.

I don't know how it would feel to have a child of yours die. Two of my son's classmates died at an early age: Andrew at thirteen and Kenny at eighteen. What greater loss is there than that? We see the boys' families in church, following their faith, serving as a great inspiration to us all. The life struggles I write about in this book are nothing compared to what these families have had to go through. What we have in common is a faith in God to help us through each day.

Looking back at over sixty-four years of my life, it has been a journey. The path I follow has been clear for me since an early age. From my parents, school, and faith community, there has always been loving guidance along the way as I grew. My struggles to stay on the path were difficult, and at times I was lost. But there was always a loving God waiting for me. My parents, my sister, and my friends were also a great support. When it comes down to it, that's what life is all about: honoring God and others.

The way I understand the meaning of life comes from Matthew 22:36–39:

> "Teacher, which is the greatest commandment in the law?"
>
> Jesus replied: "Love the Lord your God with all your soul and with all your mind. This is the first and greatest commandment. And the second is like it: Love your neighbor as yourself."

That's it, simple and direct, my marching orders in life. The Reverend Dr. Dale Turner gave us one way to carry out these commandments:

> "Give me a sense of humor, Lord.
> Give me the grace to see a joke.
> To get some pleasure out of life
> And pass it on to other folk.
> Give me sympathy and sense
> And help keep my courage high.
> Give me calm and confidence
> And, please, a twinkle in my eye."

My favorite Bible passage is from Matthew 25:40: "Truly, I say to you: Whenever you did this to one of the least of my brothers, you did it to me." I've tried to remember and live by this throughout my life. When you follow the Word of God, it can bring you great joy.

Dr. Turner wrote in one of his *Seattle Times* articles about being third. I was so inspired by what he wrote that I made business cards to reflect the message. On the front—in big, bold letters—the card says the following: **Striving to BE THIRD.** On the back, this is written:

1. God is first in my life.
2. Others second.
3. I'm third.

The movie *It's a Wonderful Life*, starring Jimmy Stewart and Donna Reed, reflects on how we all touch people's lives and influence them. Remember the character of George Bailey in the movie? He didn't realize how many lives he had affected during his time on earth. Like George, we too have helped our fellow man in so many ways but really will never know to what extent. All we can do is to keep praying and to be kind and help each other.

I wrote this book to inspire others to also follow their dreams and passions, to follow God's lead. It won't always take us in the direction we think we should be going, to the life we think we should have. Through our faith, the struggles, disappointments, and doubts can come peace. Dr. Turner wrote, "The value of Jesus's teaching is that it does not tell us how we ought to behave in every circumstance, but it describes a way of life to be worked out in the development of personal character and social relationships."

I have written about the various roles I have had throughout my life. Parking lot attendant, bellboy, son, restaurant manager, orphanage worker, brother, athlete, crisis worker, husband, father, night club manager, friend, marathon runner, psychologist, teacher, and volunteer were some of the hats I wore through the years. With mostly ups and some downs, I tried to follow the path God had set for me. Through prayer, good people around us, rolling up our sleeves and never giving up, we can all find our own path.

Through the following stories, I have tried to show how—through God's grace—it has been a fulfilling journey.

1

WORK

"Whatever you do, work at it with all your heart,
as working for the Lord, not for men"
(Col. 3:23).

My first job with a paycheck was parking cars at the age of fourteen. I was working at the Emil Motor Hotel on 5th and Spring in downtown Seattle. How could a kid so young get such a cool job driving different vehicles? It helps when your dad is managing owner of the hotel. I used to take the bus from home on the weekends to make some extra cash. Granted, you couldn't drive the cars very far in the garage—I didn't have a license at the time—but it was neat to sit behind the wheel of all those different cars. A few years after parking cars, I moved inside the hotel as a bellboy, then front desk clerk, night auditor, and head housekeeper during the summer. All these jobs gave me great experience in how to deal with customers and help meet their needs.

The Kennedy was a one-hundred-room hotel that had a lot of charm, and it was fun to work there. My dad had changed the name from the Emil Motor Hotel to the Kennedy after the first year, a good move. Dad was in the hotel on a daily basis, but I never worked directly under him. It was educational and motivational to watch him manage the hotel. He was a smart businessman and treated each dollar as if it was his last one. At the same time, he had a fondness for his employees and really got to know them.

The first two years while I was attending the University of Nevada Las Vegas, I didn't work at a job. Going to school, running track, and being on various committees at the fraternity kept me busy. During my third year at UNLV, I had a part-time job at a motel in downtown Las Vegas. The first thing you noticed when you walked into the small lobby of this motel was a huge moose head behind the counter. My childhood nickname was Moose, so I guess I was at the right place! I worked there much in the same way I had at the Kennedy. I tried to sell the customer a suite if they just came in looking for a room. Sometimes I would wheel and deal and drop the price somewhat if they would spend more for a better room. I thought I was doing a good job for the owners by making them extra money. When the owners found out, I was told just to stick with the set room rates. I can now understand how the owners felt. I guess at the time I thought I was still the owner's son.

At the end of the school year, it was time to graduate from UNLV with a bachelor of science in hotel administration. There were many hotel chains whose representatives came to campus during my senior year to interview future employees. I didn't go to any interviews because I already had a plan of what I was going to do after graduation. My best friend Ted "Newy" Newman had graduated from the University of Washington with a business degree. We decided that with our freshly printed diplomas, we would move to Hawaii and get jobs there. I wanted to get into the management side of the restaurant or hotel business, and Newy wanted to get into the management side of the retail business. I also had a letter of recommendation from the vice president of Western International Hotels (later named the Westin Hotels). What could stop two recent graduates who were motivated to set the world—well, maybe just Honolulu—on fire?

Looking back at our prediction now, I can see that while nothing stopped me, many things surely slowed me down. Newy and I arrived on the island of Oahu during the summer of 1976. We stayed at the YMCA at first before we found an apartment. Right away, I made an appointment with the assistant general manager of the Ilikai Hotel, as the letter of recommendation had instructed me to do. I was very confident that soon I would be working in some management trainee position at the beautiful Ilikai Hotel in Honolulu.

From the beginning of the interview, I had a feeling that the assistant general manager didn't want to be there and was offended by the letter, which basically told him to "get this guy a job." After a short time of looking over my resume and asking a few questions, he told me in a cold and dismissive way that he would get back to me in a week. Two weeks went by, and I hadn't yet received a call from anyone from the Ilikai. I asked my dad what to do next because I was pretty worried. He told me to call the vice president who had given me the letter of recommendation and tell him what happened. When I reached the VP, who was living in Seattle at the time, he told me to be in the assistant general manager's office at noon the next day. *Wow, that man doesn't mess around!* I remember thinking.

The next day, I went back to the assistant general manager's office in the same suit I wore the first time (I only had one suit, and who wears a suit on a regular basis in Hawaii anyway?). He appeared not to be a happy camper. He told me that he had to hire me, and he didn't like the way I had gone about it. I was offered a job as either a parking lot attendant (boy, that would be going back to square one!) or a security guard. I was shocked! I didn't mind being at the bottom of the ladder in the management trainee program, but I didn't want to be at the bottom of the ladder in the garage. I declined his offer and walked out of his office—numb.

I was now left without any connections job-wise and would have to find work a different way. I was still a college graduate; that must count for something. Over the next two months, Newy and I looked for jobs, to no avail. Newy went back to the mainland at that time, looking for greener pastures, which he did find.

I still wanted to live in Hawaii, even though money was getting thin. I found a new roommate, so that helped a lot with rent. But time was still running out. During my daily search on foot for a job in downtown Waikiki, I took a side street and came across an outdoor nightclub called Hula's. Most of the bar was situated under a giant banyan tree. It was early afternoon and the place was empty. I walked in to see if I could find someone who worked there. The owner walked out from the back and I asked him if he had any jobs available. He asked me a few general questions, then out of the blue, he asked me out for lunch. I guessed that meant he was paying, so I said, "Sure." At the end of the lunch, again out of the blue, the owner asked me if I was gay. I was speechless for a moment, then I replied, "No, is that a problem?" He said no, but he wanted me to know that Hula's was a gay bar. Would that be a problem? I replied, "No problem at all." I had never had any negative feelings toward gays, so no big deal. To be honest, the way my money was running out, the owner could have said it was a biker bar or catered to little green men from the planet Uzo, it wouldn't have mattered. I was in.

My job at Hula's was as doorman, which included checking IDs, collecting cover charges, and serving as bouncer. The term *bouncer*, I guess, comes from bouncing people out the door who don't want to leave on their own. I didn't have any hands-on experience being a bouncer (excuse the pun), but I felt I could talk someone out the door with my people skills. I found out early that it could have been a straight bar or a gay bar; if someone is totally out of it, you needed to employ a different kind of people skills. I could have used more patience on my part for breaking up a fight or showing someone out. At times I got my shirt ripped or blood on my pants. That was the biggest problem being the only sheriff in town in Dodge City. Even though fights didn't happen very often, it fell on me to take care of all fights. Most of the staff was female, so I was pretty much on my own.

Being a straight guy working in a gay bar wasn't a problem. The word got around that I wasn't interested, so the regular customers stopped asking me out. They became protective of me, especially when new folks came to the bar. I also dated one of the female staff; there wasn't too much competition around.

I was still looking for a management position during the day. After months of looking, I was hired as a floor supervisor at Fisherman's Wharf, which was a restaurant in the Spencecliff Corporation. Spencecliff had several different themed restaurants on the island. The pay was minimal, but I was excited to be in a management position. This was a great experience, working with seasoned food servers at the Wharf. I was one of the few *haoles* (white people) working at the restaurant, and I was the youngest manager. It was a very busy restaurant for lunch and dinner. As a floor supervisor, my job was to do everything that wasn't getting done. This could be clearing tables, wiping up spills, seating people, or taking customer complaints. Everyone at Fisherman's Wharf accepted me right away. I wore a white safari jacket, white pants, and white shoes. With my blond hair, I looked like Casper the Friendly Ghost.

One night at Fisherman's Wharf, the evening was finally winding down when one of my waitresses asked me to keep an eye on two young local guys who had run up a big bill and looked suspicious. They both had eaten steak and lobster, washed down with several beers. At this point, the restaurant was fairly empty when I noticed one of the guys went to the bathroom then walked out the door. After a few moments, the other guy also went to the bathroom. I was waiting around the corner to see what he would do next when, like his friend, he began walking toward the door. When he was almost at the front door, I came up behind him and yelled, "Stop!" What happened next was amazing but true. The guy actually stopped and came back with me to a table in the back of the restaurant. I told him he had two options: "Either pay the bill, or I'm going to call the police." He told me he didn't have any money. I handed him the phone and said, "Find someone." By gosh, he found someone who would come by and pay the bill! All the guests had left and also most of the staff. The last employee asked me if I wanted him to stay just in case this didn't go well. I told him I had it under control. And in a loud voice—so the dine-and-dash guy could hear—I declared, "I just have to babysit this one till I get the money."

Here I was, alone with this guy in an empty restaurant. After an hour of waiting, three of his friends came in, and they didn't look happy. Their unhappiness was not directed at their knucklehead friend but at me. The biggest of the three came right up to me with a bunch of bills in his hand and reached out to give me the money, then suddenly dropped it at my feet. That gesture upset me, so I told him to pick it up. By the grace of God, he did and handed it to me. At the same time, another guy picked up a wooden chair and raised it over his head while moving toward me. I turned to him and said,

"Put the chair down." By the grace of God, he did. They did utter some choice words to me before they left the restaurant. But they left, and I was still in one piece. They waited for me in their car in the parking lot, but I left through a side door and walked home through the park. Young and foolish comes to mind on how I handled that event. I believe my guardian angel was watching over me.

After one year at Fisherman's Wharf, I was promoted to assistant manager at a small coffee shop on the other side of the island. The night before beginning my new job at Tops Kanoe, the employees at Fisherman's Wharf had a going-away party for me. It went into the early morning, with many drinks shared by all. At the end of the night, I was thrown into the pool with my clothes on, which was the traditional ending when people leave to go to another restaurant. I had to be at the new job at 7:00 a.m. Even with only a few hours' sleep, I told everyone I would make it. Well, I was two hours late, and when I walked in, I was really embarrassed. The manager smiled and said that was all right because someone had called to say I was going to be late. How did they know?

Mostly local people came to the coffee shop, and you really got a flavor of the Hawaiian culture. Next stop was another coffee shop on the main drag of Waikiki. I worked several 10:00 p.m. to 10:00 a.m. shifts. From all the clubs and bars in the area, lots of people came to the restaurant after a night of drinking. Most of the time, things were fine. Once in a while, though, the night got interesting. A few times, I had to run out the door when customers dashed out without paying. I never caught anyone (maybe that was a good thing!), but I sure tried. Several times I had to lift customers' heads from their meals when they passed out. I'll always remember the guy with a long beard who passed out in a plate of spaghetti. He tried to clean himself up when I woke him, but I guess everyone knew what he ate when he walked out the door.

The Canterbury Coffee House and Tavern was the last Spencecliff restaurant where I worked. The manager there was Keith Matsumoto, and I worked with two other assistant managers, Les Mokuledua and Roy Spenser. The chef was "Yama" Yamashita. We had the privilege of opening up a brand new restaurant. We worked together setting things up for two months before Canterbury opened. We developed policy, pricing, staffing, and everything else underneath the sun. It was a great experience to learn how much work it took to open up a large restaurant. When the doors opened up for our customers, it was an exciting day, seeing all the employees in their English-style uniforms eager to get working.

Having the least amount of experience among the assistant managers, I got the wonderful graveyard shifts, which usually ran from 10:00 p.m. to 8:00 or 10:00 a.m., five days a week. As a manager, you always want the restaurant to be busy for many reasons. The most important reason is to make money for the company. Other reasons would be when there are more customers, your wait staff are busy, and when they are busy, they're happy because they're making more tips. When the restaurant is hopping, everyone gets into a rhythm, all are working as a big team; it's a thing of beauty. Canterbury was a unique and brand new restaurant. We were usually very busy. I was the only manager on duty, which I liked because I could run the show. My job was to fill in anywhere needed and to keep the customers happy. Looking back at my experience at Canterbury, at times I pushed my staff too hard.

I remember it was a busy Friday night and one of my food servers was extremely busy, flying around, doing her best. Right in the middle of this busy evening, I got on her case for not putting a piece of pie down on the guest's table the proper way. Looking back at the incident, was I serious? I should have been telling her she was doing a good job trying to manage all her tables. Through experience and feedback (that waitress wasn't happy with me), I learned to loosen up more but still run an organized restaurant.

I noticed a want ad while working at Canterbury for a manager position at Annabelle's in the Westin Ilikai Hotel. Even though I liked my job, I wanted to move up from an assistant manager position to be a full manager. The Ilikai was the same place where I had been offered the security or parking attendant job. I hoped that the same assistant general manager was not there.

Annabelle's was a disco on the top floor of the hotel. It had been open for just six months and had already gone through two managers. I got the interview with the food and beverage director, Tony Cherone. He interviewed me in his office and even came over to Canterbury when I was working. At the end of the second interview, he told me that I got the job and that he wanted to introduce me to the assistant general manager. I was thinking, *Oh no, I hope it isn't the same guy!* It was! He appeared not to know me, so we shook hands. And he welcomed me aboard. The assistant general manager left the hotel shortly after I arrived. To this day, I don't know if he knew me or not; I did wear the same suit all three times we met.

Annabelle's was a beautiful nightspot for dancing. When the era of disco came, the hotel management felt that they could get rid of the live bands and save a lot of money by having just a DJ. The bands drew a large early crowd of mostly middle-aged regulars with some tourists. With the conception of Annabelle's and a DJ spinning the records, most of the regulars did not come back because they wanted live music and didn't want to dance to taped light disco music from 5:00 to 9:00 p.m. At 9:00 p.m., when the DJ came in to raise the tempo, the club was only a quarter full. At 9:00 p.m. we started charging cover charge, and the late-night younger crowd wanted a roomful of people, with lots of action. Hotel guests didn't have to pay the cover charge, so we got some people from there but the place still looked empty. Even though Annabelle's was thirty stories up, on top of the hotel with a view of Diamond Head, it was still not a "happening place." We lost most of our early evening crowd, and our late crowd was slow to moderate. The hotel advertised and gave out free food and snacks from 5:00 to 9:00 p.m. without much success. The nights really dragged on, especially during the weekdays, and if it wasn't for the hotel guests and the Japanese tourists, Annabelle's would have been a ghost town.

After being open for one year and with me serving as the manager for a few months, we needed to do some things differently. After providing feedback to upper management, we problem-solved a new format for Annabelle's. First, I found a person older than your average DJ who knew the music of the Big Band era, the '50s, and the '60s. Pam was a singer in various clubs and had great knowledge of those eras. So Pam and I went out record shopping for the "5:00

p.m. to 9:00 p.m." crowd, and out went the taped mild disco music. Pam was very personable and picked up the art of DJing quickly. My hope was to bring back the regulars with danceable music for the early evening slot.

This was a good start, but we needed something else to really send this off. A few days later, the new assistant general manager came up to Annabelle's for a drink after work. We were talking about how to get more people in, especially between 5:00 and 9:00 p.m. Out of the blue, he asked me, "Why don't you lower your drink prices for standard drinks?" I replied, "If we do it, the prices really have to go down to really create a big impact." Currently the standard drinks were $2.00. Mr. Hollander thought for a moment, then said, "Why don't you lower it to $1.00?" The first thought that came into my mind was *he's crazy!* But after thinking it over, I changed the word "crazy" to brilliant.

Once the new price change was approved, we started a three-week advertising of our new happy-hour format with the Big Band sound and golden oldies played by our DJ Pam, all at just $1.00 for standard drinks for four hours. We advertised on four radio stations and in the local paper. We changed our first class well (the liquor we used for standard drinks) to our standard bar well that we used in other outlets. This saved us over $500 a month.

On July 16, 1979, we began the new approach with a hope and a prayer. It didn't take long to see that the lower priced drinks were bringing our regulars back and attracting lots of new local customers. The following breakdown proves the point.

July 23, Monday			July 24, Tuesday	
Standard	$1.00	84%	$1.00	80%
Call	$2.00	8%	$2.00	11%
Exotics	$3.25	8%	$3.25	9%

August 17, Friday was the best night ever in total sales:

$2,736	Liquor	
495	Cover ($5.00)	
$3,231		

Happy hour at Annabelle's was the place to be! First and foremost, any business needs a steady flow of steady customers, which we now had. Add to that our hotel guests and tourists in general who came up for the view. Together, they made it a popular place. Another aspect of a busy happy hour was when 9:00 p.m. came around and we started the cover charge, the place was packed with people dancing and just hanging out. This made it more appealing for the late night crowd.

Through the months, I had a ladies' night with free cover for the ladies and a drink special for all. Disco dance lessons began every Sunday, with a good response. Business was good, and we were now one of the hottest nightspots in Honolulu.

In January 1980, we now stayed open till 4:00 a.m., reduced the cover charge from $5.00 to $3.00 per person, and increased the standard drinks during happy hour to $1.25. Staying open till 4:00 a.m. really increased our sales on Friday and Saturday nights.

When I was in Seattle for a vacation, I went to a nightspot that had a lip-sync contest. Contestants dressed up as the artist whose song they were going to perform. There was a Michael Jackson, a Madonna, and a Johnny Cash, among others. The show was entertaining, and the crowd really got into it. From my point of view, this club was making good money on a weekday night and entertainment was almost free with a $50—cash prize for the winner. It seemed a lot of fun for everyone, but most importantly, it appeared to be making money.

I brought this concept back to management and got some marketing money to advertise it. I got a pair of big red lips, Mick Jagger style, and named the contest Lip It. We advertised Lip It in the newspaper and on the radio. The contestants would pick the artist they wanted to lip-sync to, dress up like the entertainer, and hit it with their best shot (Pat Benatar pun intended). On opening night, I didn't know for sure if we would have anyone show up to the program. You never know until they're actually there. The show must go on, so I figured out a way to accomplish this even if there weren't any Lip It contestants. Some friends and I would perform! My DJ was Dolly Parton; my assistant manager, his girlfriend, and friends were a hard rock band called Metallica; and I performed as the Blues Brother with three female back-up singers who also were my horn players. At least we had three acts ready if no one wanted to perform!

With one hour before the show, two performers showed up (a Michael Jackson and a solo AC/DC act). Then minutes before the contest, Donna Summer showed up (not the real one, which would have been nice). The crowd appeared to really like the performers and cheered everyone on. I had a lot of fun being the Blues Brother with my Blue Sisters. The coolest thing about my act was that I could bounce around, give a soulful performance, and never have to sing a note. Being employees, we weren't in the running for the money prizes: First was paid $100. Second was paid $50, and third earned some free drinks. Lip It proved to be a really successful promotion, bringing in added revenue on a Tuesday night.

I worked as Annabelle's manager for five years. For the last two years, we were still doing great business, but my heart wasn't 100 percent into it. I was doing volunteer work as a Big Brother of Hawaii, then worked on the Suicide/Crisis Hotline after work—the 12 midnight to 8:00 a.m. shift once a week. I also began taking some classes at the University of Hawaii in psychology during the day. Through prayer and reflection, I felt myself being led in another direction.

During my fourth year at Annabelle's, I had my annual review by the new food and beverage manager. I thought I should have gotten higher scores than "good" and more scores in the "excellent" range. The F&B director said he would talk it over with his boss. They changed my scores to mostly *excellents*, which would also increase my salary. I felt recognized for the success of Annabelle's.

A few weeks later, a report came in that changed things again. The Ilikai had recently hired two spotters, who came into the hotel to check up on the services and running of the hotel. These spotters were unknown to all the staff except the general manager. They used all the facilities of the Ilikai, then wrote a report on how each area did. Annabelle's did not do well. The couple who were the spotters reported that some of the staff were unfriendly and service was slow. They stated that there wasn't any presence of management on the floor and things looked disorganized. The food and beverage manager went over the negative report with me. He then told me that my evaluation would go back to what it was originally. He had the tone of "I told you so" in his talk with me. When I was leaving our meeting and heading for the door, he yelled, "And get a haircut."

This experience took me down a few notches on how well I thought Annabelle's was doing. After praying on it and reflection, I knew what had to be done. I had to tighten up the ship. That mostly meant that I just needed to spend more time at Annabelle's. This was a good lesson for me because it taught me that you can't rest on your success but must keep seeking improvement. Also my heart told me that psychology and pursuing graduate school was at the top of my list. Before I could leave Annabelle's, I needed to take care of business first.

The next spotters' report was spotless. With that mission accomplished, it was time to move on. My last day at Annabelle's was a wonderful experience. Several customers gave me a lei, a Hawaiian tradition. The staff pooled their money together and got me a ring made out of a horseshoe with a diamond in it. I didn't have to manage that night because I was the guest of honor. It was very touching to say goodbye to so many great people. Five years at Annabelle's went fast but will always be in my memories.

The next weekend, I was working at the Hawaii State Mental Hospital as a nursing assistant. I was out of my suit, now wearing jeans and a polo shirt. My job was exactly like what you might have seen in the movies: the guys in the white coats. I thought all future psychologists first had to learn the ropes at the local mental hospital. So I did everything from emptying waste baskets to escorting patients to their appointments. The nursing assistants spent the most time with the patients. Where they were, we were there too. The psychologists saw the patients only on a limited basis, and the nurses were away from the patients many times during the day. The nurses had a lot to do, from getting everyone's medication ready to charting the events of the day to running groups. I really admired these nurses who really had the best interests of the patients at heart.

I worked for one year at Hawaii State Hospital, and I met some interesting people. I was a floater, moving around to different units when staff were on vacation or were out sick. I remember one day when I first worked on the criminally insane unit, a patient walked up to me with his hand out and introduced himself as the Waikiki sniper. He said that he had killed six people and was on the front page of the newspaper. I just smiled, nodded my head, and kept moving. I remember another time right before I was going onto the unit, we were having our briefing for the upcoming shift. I noticed one of the nursing assistants was leaving the unit with a bloody nose. He told me that he had been hit in the face by one of the patients who didn't like white people (*haoles*). I asked the nursing assistant to point this patient out to me because I hadn't worked that unit very often. When I went on the locked unit, I always kept an eye on Slugger. One time in the evening, I had to interact with him, and the subject of boxing came up. He was a knowledgeable fan as was I, so we had something in common to talk about. It was a blessing. I interacted with Slugger through the night on the subject of boxing without getting into a fight!

Through, during, and after graduate school, the theme of my jobs was always to serve others. That's where I believe God was directing me. From working and living with brain-injured adults to teaching at Edmonds Community College and Puget Sound Christian College, I really enjoyed interacting with others and learning so much from them.

After coming back to the United States from Romania with my beautiful bride, I needed to finish the post-doctoral hours supervised by a psychologist so that I could be licensed in Washington. I was lucky to have a past supervisor, Lisa Kahn, who was working at the University of Washington Child Development Clinic who got me in. I was thankful for the experience, but the pay there was low—so I had to find another job. I began working for Compass Health in the children's crisis team. This was an entry level position for those with a master's degree; the pay wasn't great, but I got into the profession to work with kids and families. So I took the job. I began working at Compass in 1994. My plan was to work there for a few years while looking for a more psychologist-like job (my plan, not God's). I held the Compass job until 2009, for fifteen years! Compass discontinued the children's crisis team during that time and blended it into the adult crisis team.

Being a team leader on the children's crisis team involved going into homes, ERs, or schools, wherever a child 17 years old or younger was in crisis. The location in need would call the Care Crisis Line. The person there would determine whether or not to send me out, then they would page me to go to any place in Snohomish County. If it was a child's home, I would have a crisis aide come with me, thus the name crisis team. If the outreach was to a school or ER, I would go solo. Of the thousands of outreaches I went to, each had a unique story. Many of the children came from a disruptive home where violence and drug/alcohol addiction were common. These children naturally acted out these behaviors at home, school, and in the community. When the situation got to a breaking point, the child was sent to the ER.

Sometimes, the children were so broken down from the events of their lives that they became suicidal. One of my roles was to determine if the child was safe to go home. If it appeared that they were a danger to themselves, we needed to get them into a hospital. This process could take hours, and after all the time put into it, we still might not find a bed for the child. I needed to work with the family on a crisis plan to keep the child safe. I enjoyed speaking with the kids who were going through a hard time and we tried to get their crisis under control. The parents of the child in crisis were an interesting group. Some were genuinely concerned about their child, while other parents were angry and blaming. Others were in denial, shock, or bothered by being called because of their child.

I learned through the years to listen and not to be judgmental. I remember a statement made by the late Reverend Dale Turner that has stuck with me through the years: "Be kind. Everyone you know is carrying a heavy burden."

Being a crisis worker was a joy in many ways. First, and most importantly, this was where God wanted me to be. I knew this through prayer. Second, I really enjoyed working with the kids and families. Third, I could work two sixteen-hour shifts and one eight-hour day and have my forty hours done. I could be around the house more watching my son Ted as he grew up, which was priceless. During those years with Compass Health, I could also do some community service. I volunteered at Hospice of Seattle with the Safe Crossing program. My duties entailed being with children when one of their parents was dying and in hospice care. I just hung out with them, not as a psychologist but as a friend.

I also had the chance to volunteer at a day center that served the homeless in downtown Seattle. I was the resident counselor there. The homeless people taught me a lot about how to be resilient. It was an honor to hear their stories. Most came from traumatic backgrounds but their hope shined brightly. Several were mentally ill and needed a place where they could be safe. Many were in recovery and looking for someone to help them get into services.

I also volunteered at Operation Nightwatch, which was in downtown Seattle. Operation Nightwatch tried to get people a place to sleep for the night. Nightwatch opened up at 10:00 p.m. to 1:00 a.m. every night. I helped prepare hot meals for the people who were hungry and had no place to go. At the beginning I stayed behind the counter serving food. After a week, one of the senior volunteers told me to go out from the counter and just talk to people. I guess in some ways I felt I was different. I found out that the homeless had a heart and soul, just like everyone else. Many had some bad luck and others came from some rough backgrounds. I wasn't a therapist, trying to help with a problem, but just another human being sharing with another human being. We are all the same species.

When Monica and I settled down in Edmonds, one of the first things we did was to find a Catholic church. We went to a few and decided on Holy Rosary of Edmonds. After a few years attending there, I heard that the pastor, Father Ken Haydock, recently had a counselor working at the church to help with the psychological needs of the parish. The counselor didn't last long because she didn't have the experience to handle the wide emotional needs of a church with over 1,500 families. I was fortunate to get the job in 2002 and have been working there ever since.

This was an innovative move by the pastor. Usually priests would refer their parishioners for mental health services to Catholic

Community Services (CCS). Father Haydock has always been a priest who reaches out to the needs of his parish and community. In his eyes, just like in the teachings of Jesus, everyone is welcomed and important. At CCS, even though it's a wonderful community service, it could take weeks for the person to get in. You also didn't know what type of expertise your assigned CCS counselor had. Thus I began a relationship with the community of Holy Rosary, and I got to see firsthand all the helpful things Father Haydock does behind the scenes.

I began working at Holy Rosary one day a week, which evolved to two days a week. I remember seeing eleven clients in a row one day. I wouldn't recommend it on a regular basis, but I really felt I was doing something that was fulfilling to me and serving a need at Holy Rosary. The experience increased my faith in so many ways. Parishioners wanted their spiritual beliefs used in part of their treatment. I got to work with students and families of the school. Through the years, I must have seen close to a thousand people from Holy Rosary, and that was just on a part-time basis, which in the last five years has gone back to me being there once a week.

Does this mean Holy Rosary has an overabundance of mental health needs? I don't think so. Everyone needs a little help once in a while. With the grace of God, Father Haydock had the foresight to see this, but most importantly, he did something about it.

In the summer of 2016, Father Haydock, after twenty years of service at Holy Rosary, went to Saint Bridget Parish. He was replaced by Father Vincent, who brought a great amount of energy and passion to his new church. He mentioned that his main job was to get his parishioners to heaven. That sounded good to me, because we all need all the help we can get. Father Vincent is a wonderful storyteller and educator who weaves this knowledge with the scripture readings. Each of his homilies is an adventure with a deep sense of holiness. Father Vincent also carried on the tradition set by Father Haydock on serving the counseling needs at Holy Rosary.

When I was working on the crisis team, my job was to stabilize the situation at the child's home, school, or at the ER. If the child didn't need to be hospitalized, they would go home with their parent(s). One of the recommendations I would give the family was to get into counseling. Through the years, I heard it wasn't that easy just to get their child into counseling. Many families didn't have insurance for mental health; others could qualify for DSHS (Department of Social and Health Services), but that would take time.

For families in crisis, time is one thing they don't have. The ones who had insurance were in better shape, but it could still take weeks for them to be seen by a counselor. The small group of families who could afford the $100-plus per hour usually could be seen right away. So where could a lot of these families go? Nowhere. The community mental health agencies were trying their best to meet the need, but the demand was bigger than the resources. It was frustrating for us in emergency services. We could help stabilize the situation for the moment, but in the long run not much would be accomplished without ongoing counseling.

Frustrated when I could not get families the help they needed right away, my work as a crisis worker had a big influence on what would happen several years down the road. The movie *Patch Adams* was another major influence on me. Based on a true story, Patch Adams, played by actor Robin Williams, was a medical student who felt his patients were much more than just their diseases. He got to know the patients at the hospital far beyond their illnesses. Patch had a vision of patient-centered health care for everyone, even if they couldn't afford it. During medical school, he opened up a free clinic to treat minor medical issues, but mostly it was a place anyone could come who was lonely, scared, and had nowhere else to go. Years later, in 2015, I had the chance to meet the real Patch Adams at a lecture/workshop he held. There were only fifty of us, which made a very intimate setting. It was truly a blessing to hear from a man who travels 300 days a year in a clown suit. He has been to seventy-nine countries, spreading joy with his humor and service to others. Patch has a special place in his heart for children and has been to several orphanages around the world.

When I walked out of the movie theater in 1998, I was inspired to do something like Patch Adams did with mental health counseling. Through these two experiences, I told myself, *If I ever have the chance to set up a clinic to serve people with mental health needs with nowhere to go, I will do it.* Prayer put these two experiences—children's crisis worker and watching the movie *Patch Adams*—into a reality to help others. Without God's direction, none of this would be possible.

Affordable Counseling (AC) came to reality in 2008. It was set up for anyone who didn't have insurance, who had too high a deductible, or who was going through a difficult time financially. The fee of a fifty-minute session would be between $5 and $20; the client would tell me what they could afford to pay. It took a lot of prayer and six months of searching to find the home of Affordable Counseling. I looked at several locations around the Edmonds, Lynnwood, even the Everett area. Everything was too expensive. I really felt that this was God's idea that Affordable would come about. I kept looking and praying. There was a two-story commercial building three minutes from my house. It was on my list but I hadn't gotten to it, maybe because the outside didn't look the most appealing. There were two large office spaces available but again, the rent was too high.

As I told the landlord, the rent was too high and began walking away, she mentioned there might be one more space to look at. It was the first space after you came through the front entrance. The office was smaller than the others and was used as a storage room with ladders, paint cans, and had an old carpet. My first reaction was "No way!" as the place was a mess. When the landlady told me the rent, my next reaction was "Can you clean it up a bit?" She did. My wife, Monica, was a great help in finding reasonably priced furniture to put in. I wanted to get a good price on the furnishings without having it look cheap.

I opened up Affordable Counseling in February of 2008. The mission statement of the clinic was the Prayer of St. Francis of Assisi. The prayer really spoke to what we're trying to do at AC:

"Lord make me an instrument of your peace.
Where there is hatred, let me sow love.
Where there is injury, pardon.
Where there is doubt, faith.

Where there is despair, hope.
Where there is darkness, light.
Where there is sadness, joy.
O Divine Master, grant that
I may not so much seek
To be consoled, as to console.
To be understood, as to understand.
To be loved, as to love.
For it is in giving that we receive.
It is in pardoning that we are pardoned.
It is in dying that we are born to eternal life."
                                            —*St. Francis of Assisi*

A story I heard many years ago also reminded me of what we're trying to accomplish at AC:

"A small boy was throwing starfish that were washed up on the sand back into the ocean. There were thousands of them but the boy was patiently throwing them back into the water, one by one. An adult came by and asked the boy what he was doing. He stated, 'I'm helping the starfish.' The adult replied, 'What is the point? You cannot make a difference, there are so many starfish all over the shore.' The boy smiled and said, 'It makes a difference to the ones that make it back to the ocean.'"

I began working at Affordable Counseling on Tuesdays and a half-day on Wednesdays. I was still at Compass Health and Holy Rosary. There was no formal advertising at AC; it was all by word of mouth. Spending fifteen years going on outreaches to the ER and into schools with the Children's Crisis Team got my name around. AC was a place where social workers, care crisis line workers, school staff, and other professionals could refer people. The word spread that anyone could be seen at AC for what they could afford, without producing any documents or W2s on their income. They would be seen by a clinical psychologist. Not a bad deal! After a few weeks, the phone began ringing off the hook. Within two months, now seeing clients also on Mondays, I had to begin a waiting list.

One of the goals I wanted to accomplish at AC was to see people within a few days after they called. I was asking the Lord to send me an intern to help out with the demand. I wanted someone with experience, maybe a doctoral student. A few days later I got a call from Mary Rawson, who was on the adult emergency service team at Compass Health. She fit in nicely on the days I wasn't there. Mary Rawson was with me for a year and did a tremendous job.

I soon realized another therapist was needed. I prayed if it was God's will, I could sure use another person. Shortly after the prayers, Michelle Mann, who worked in the outpatient building of Compass, called, and my second clinician was in place. The phone kept ringing, which really showed a need in the community for low-cost counseling. Without any insurance forms to fill out and with minimal paperwork, clients could be seen quickly. When the office across the hall opened up, Affordable Counseling expanded to two offices. This second office also had a smaller room that was set up for a children's treatment playroom. Another area was set up with a large table so we could meet as a group and discuss cases. With clients paying between $5 and $20, with three therapists working using two offices, I could pay the rent and other expenses.

To make this happen, the interns do not receive any stipend for their work. They get to see a wide range of clients, receive direct and group supervision once a week, and obtain the needed clinical hours to graduate. For most of the interns, it has become more than just another requirement to check off for school. They have become a part of the spirit of AC, seeing clients who have limited or no mental health resources. The interns know they are needed to serve the community from the first day at AC. Their energy helps me keep going.

When I left Compass Health two years into Affordable Counseling, I could take a small salary. I considered looking for a second office space up north, Everett or Marysville, because several clients had come from that direction. I even inquired about possible locations but couldn't find anything that would fit the budget. One night, my wife Monica said, "Why don't you open up another office where you're at? They will come," and they did. Currently, as of 2017, we have three offices onsite and six interns.

As I mentioned before, Mary Rawson was the first intern. She was also an art therapist and an expert on attention-deficit/hyperactivity disorder or ADHD; she ran a group at AC for women with ADHD. It couldn't have been a better fit with her as the first student at AC. Mary Rawson became the first licensed psychologist of the group.

My second therapist was Michelle, who was with me for three years. Michelle worked a full-time job during the day, then worked at AC from 5:00 to 9:00 p.m. three nights a week and on Saturdays. Dedicated, experienced, and a great finder of mental health resources, Michelle went on to get her doctorate.

Brina was full of energy and very invested with all her clients. She is a person with many talents, from accomplished pianist to skilled editor who has helped countless students with their dissertations. Brina has used her experiences in many areas of life to really make an impact with her clients. She went on to get her doctorate.

Anders, originally from Ireland, brought a different perspective to the group. His humor and his laid-back style was a benefit to his clients. On occasion, if a teen client was interested in rock 'n' roll, Anders would bring in his electric guitar and do a few licks. He also went on and earned his doctorate.

Angela was a good fit at AC, already with solid therapy skills. Her positive attitude and gift for working with couples helped make AC grow.

Aggie, originally from Poland, came with a solid background working with various agencies. She was the first to start the tradition of taking group photos of the interns who were leaving.

Shannon was a case worker before joining AC and did a good job for her clients.

Roy was a pastor of a church while still doing his internship at AC. Roy was a big Dallas Cowboys fan, but we didn't hold that against him. He was a dedicated therapist who really had his clients' best interests at heart.

Ann had a writing background and wrote a wonderful book for teens on dealing with a family member with mental illness. She learned the therapy ropes quickly and really had a lot of compassion toward her clients.

Mary was conscientious and serious about her profession. She did an excellent job on running a group for women on guilt and shame.

Ashley did a wonderful job with her clients. She especially had a great feel for working with teenage girls.

Carol was the most experienced of all the interns who came through AC. She already had a flourishing practice in the Tri-Cities area of eastern Washington. Carol did a tremendous job with her couples in therapy. Her presentation of cases during our group meetings was informative and creative.

Bryce, local ER social worker and ex-schoolteacher, brought a lot of knowledge to AC. His gentle way and experience to help clients move past from where they were was a huge asset and had his clients speaking highly of him.

Beth already had her master's and was a successful outreach clinician who did assessments in the ER to see if a client should be detained to a hospital. She spent a year without pay to see clients at AC. Beth just wanted to improve her therapy skills, which she did, but also touched the lives of her clients.

Renee was full of energy and was a sponge for learning. She learned quickly and was a big benefit to her clients, especially couples. Using her past Microsoft experience, she was the driving force of creating a new and improved website for AC.

Kayce was also full of energy, with ideas and questions. She brought that energy to all her clients, especially the children she worked with. Kayce also did a wonderful job working with the parents, which requires lots of patience.

Jane came to AC with lots of worldly experience, which included working with the Peace Corps. She built a good relationship with her clients and was there through some difficult times. Jane, using her life experiences, could keep things under control during intense times in therapy with even having a laugh or two.

Todd came to AC from having the past experience of being a pastor. His calling to be of service to others was really apparent in his counseling. Todd has a great deal of compassion for his clients and has done tremendous work with couples. He transitioned nicely from pulpit to therapy couch.

I got a call out of the blue from Monica, who was in a master's program online for counseling. What was unique in this situation was that she wasn't looking for client hours but just wanted to volunteer any way she could. I was at first hesitant because I have never received a request from a student to help out at AC without any school requirements or to gain a certain amount of counseling hours toward licensure. Monica was great, helping us with copying and compiling AC data to see how many clients have been seen and other demographics. She is also quite an artist. When the time came for Monica to begin her internship, I asked her to join the AC team and start seeing real clients. She said that she was ready for the challenge but was a little nervous because she would be running with the big dogs (working in collaboration with other therapists at AC). Monica fit in nicely and became a member of the pack.

Gabe brought a solid background of working with youth and families to AC. His creativity, warmth, and genuine desire to serve others made him a nice addition. When Gabe finished his internship, he gave me a beautiful walking stick he had made himself, with the word "Faith" carved into the handle. He chose that word for me because I always had faith in his abilities as a clinician, even when he didn't.

Kristen came to AC with various talents from group home counselor for teenage moms to providing advocacy for domestic violence victims. She hit the ground running, seeing a wide array of people in a short period of time. Kristen did a great job with some challenging couples and clients with post-traumatic stress disorder. Even through some tense times, her clinical skills, bright smile, and humor were always there.

Alissa worked in the L'Arche Community, which serves mentally and physically handicapped residents. Her understanding of the suffering of others gave her a deep sense of compassion toward her clients. Going through a lot of physical pain herself while at AC didn't affect her positive attitude or the outstanding work she did, especially with young girls.

Grace came at a time when we really needed the help. We had a short waitlist but the calls kept coming in. She got right to work and did a wonderful job. I really enjoyed her thirst for knowledge.

Jonathan did an amazing job of balancing the needs of the many clients he saw in a week; he worked three ten-hour shifts. He has great insight and takes his time to really understand each of his clients. To relieve some of the pressure of his heavy caseload, Jonathan liked to talk about fishing with me. He had some good stories and really got me hooked (pun intended).

Sarah is full of energy and brightens up her surroundings. The clients really feel that they are the most important people in the world when they see her. Sarah was ready to take on any challenges that came her way and used several creative interventions to connect with her clients.

Sam, who worked Saturdays, was one of my weekend warriors. He is a calm, confident, and hardworking clinician who will jump in when needed. Sam has helped a wide array of clients. It was fun talking football with him even though he is a Michigan and Detroit Lions fan.

What kinds of clients are seen at AC? As I mentioned before, most of the clients we see have a lower income level. For the people who have state insurance, it has been difficult to find a therapist who takes that coverage. For others, the deductible is too high. It is gratifying to hear from potential clients on the phone that they were so happy to find AC because they have been looking for affordable counseling for months and had tried several places to no avail. The people who call are just like anyone else. Currently they are going through some difficult times financially and are really being slowed down by what they are going through mentally and physically.

Through the last eight years, many wonderful stories have come out of AC. Naturally, because of confidentiality, I can't name any of the clients who have touched our lives so much. I would, however, like to share a few stories from the hundreds of clients who have impacted us at AC.

One of my first clients had to take two buses to get to counseling. She was an older lady on a tight budget, suffering from depression. At the end of the session, she handed over five dollars to pay. What really touched my heart was that the payment was all in coins in a plastic bag. The woman asked me if I wanted to count it to be sure it was correct. I told her it was all right; I knew she had the right amount. She probably saved all her nickels, dimes, and quarters just to have one session with me, very humbling.

I had a gentleman in therapy who was a hardworking janitor and, at times, had to sleep in his car due to finances. He came in around Christmastime to the office, carrying a plant. He gave us the plant and a sealed envelope. We began chatting a little, but he appeared nervous and in a rush. When I began to open up the envelope, he said he had to leave and rushed out the door. When I opened up the envelope, there was a Christmas card and inside was $70. A holiday tip, so to speak. I believe the client sensed that I would try to give the money back, so he got out as fast as possible, almost running out the door. Now what to do? He wasn't scheduled for an upcoming appointment, and I was left with this money, which he could clearly not afford to give out. And I couldn't accept anyway. After speaking with my interns, it was decided to use the money for a painting to put in the office. Two interns volunteered to pick out the painting—one with conservative tastes, the other with abstract tastes. The result: a fine painting for one of the treatment rooms. When the man came back several months later, I showed him what we had done with the money he gave us. He seemed pleased.

As a psychologist, I have noticed that many of my clients will try to remember information that has been said in session to help them during their day. One woman told me she had devised a way of remembering some important points said in session, especially in times of doubt.

"Dr. Baird, I have a way to remember some of the key points that were said in session," she mentioned one day in therapy. "You know the term 'WWJD?' 'What Would Jesus Do?' I think of something similar when I think of you. I think of WWBS."

I must admit I was stunned when I heard this, and it was hard to keep a straight face. My client explained, "I think of WWBS when I have to make an important decision or I am fighting an impulse: What Would Baird Say?"

Now that has a nice flow to it.

Another woman whom I had been seeing in therapy for over a year had been struggling with mental illness for several years. Some days were extremely difficult, other days much better. She never gave up, and her faith helped her through each day. Being a single woman, living by herself, many times it gets lonely. Through the months we discovered different ways she could get out more and interact with others: social interactions, volunteering, a part-time job. She began trying to be more social, but most of the time, she just couldn't get out of her apartment where the darkness really sets in for her.

One session, she told me of having had a cat many years ago that was her best friend. After hearing that, you didn't need a PhD to ask the question, "Why don't you get a cat?" The idea had crossed her mind, but the $100 fee was well beyond her price range. Then there was the damage deposit.

"No," she said, "I don't have the money for a cat because, most times, I have just enough money to make it to the end of the month."

When I told her that AC would pay for the cat and the first few months for food, she looked at me in shock. She asked me if what I just told her was true or was she hearing voices. After I told her it was true, she asked if she could dance. My client got up from her chair and began dancing around in a tight circle with her arms raised up to the sky, chanting in a singsong tone, "I'm getting a cat. I'm getting a cat."

During the next week, she did the research on where to find a cat that had been given up for adoption. We found two clinics that had cats that were rescued due to various circumstances. Everything looked good, then a curve ball came our way: The damage deposit was $350. She even asked the landlord if she could pay an extra $50 a month down for the deposit (the $50 would come out of her already low-food budget). That idea was turned down. I hated to do it, but I told her that AC could not put up the money for the damage deposit. She was disappointed about not getting her cat, but said she understood.

The next day, I was feeling bad about the cat situation. I ran the story by my wife Monica just to let out some of my frustrations. After hearing the whole story, she said in a calm voice, "Can I give you my opinion on this?" Getting the green light, she said, "What would you do if a family member needed five hundred dollars that would change their life? Or how about a friend, or how about someone you hardly knew?"

"To have a major impact on someone's life for five hundred dollars," I said, "that was a no-brainer. Of course it's worth five hundred dollars."

"Well?" she replied.

I didn't just marry a beautiful lady, but also a wise woman. The client got her cat, and it has really changed her life. She answers the phone now by saying, "Kitty-Cat Central, may I help you?"

I have worked with several men at AC. Many are told to go to counseling or else by their wife or girlfriend. Others are court-ordered to attend counseling. Many of these men I call my "angry guys." They come in mad at the world. If we can get past the blaming and resentment, great strides can be made. What you usually find in the journey is a hidden little boy who has been hurt deeply as a child. I enjoy working with these men, even though many don't want to be there initially. Once they understand that they have the power to get what they want without using controlling behavior and yelling and screaming, their relationship has a chance to improve.

Once a month, I usually have a guest come in to speak to us during our group time. These professionals have been very informative in their areas of expertise. I invited a counselor who worked at the county jail to share his experience. Ed told us one day at work, he was called to see an inmate who was out of control. The inmate was housed in a section of the jail where the troublemakers lived. When

Ed arrived, the inmate was shackled and quite upset. It was difficult for Ed to carry on his risk assessment with all the inmate's yelling. When Ed asked him if he was in counseling—and if he was, what was the name of the therapist?—the inmate stopped screaming. Ed reported that what the inmate said next sounded like he was doing an endorsement for a commercial. In a clear and booming voice, he announced: "My counselor is Dr. Jeff Baird." I think this angry guy needs a few more sessions.

One of the main reasons I wanted to be a psychologist was to work with children, teens, and families. Most of my internship sites involved working with kids. I really enjoy working with this population because it's challenging and always has other people involved. When you see a child or a teen, their parents, siblings, school, or other important people in their life all make up the big picture of who this person is. Being a parent myself, I understand the joys and frustrations of parenting. I can relate to the general thinking of parents that if my child just did it this way (translation: my way), everything would be all right. My job is to understand where the child or teen is coming from and what they feel could be helpful; then, after gaining information from different areas of the child or teen's life, I must try to blend the parents' concerns and the child or teen's wants together to achieve success. And all the time, while I am working with the kiddo, I focus on building on their strengths and tapping into their passions.

I remember getting a phone call from a lady who wanted to get into counseling to look at some grief issues concerning a family member who had died seven years ago. When I asked her if she had received any past counseling concerning the death, she said she did, but it wasn't very good and the counselor really didn't understand the grief process. I told her I was sorry she had that experience, and I believe we could help her here. The woman then said that she had received counseling at AC a few years ago. *Oops*, I thought, *now what to do?* I told her that the intern whom she saw meant well but probably didn't have a lot of experience in that area. I told her I would be happy to see her because I had a lot of experience dealing with grief. The lady replied, "The counselor I saw was you." *Oh!* I was speechless for a moment. My mind was racing. I could give her to an intern, but it could be that there is more going on than grief. I didn't want to set up any of my clinicians for a possible complex case. I believe that the Holy Spirit came in to guide me at that moment. I apologized again to her and said if she gave me another chance, I would do a better job. She agreed, and an appointment time was set up.

I reviewed the notes of our last three sessions and nothing jumped off the page, so I thought I would listen intently to her during the session and then ask her how the session went and how I could help her. At the end of the session, I asked her these questions and she replied that the session was fine, but that I still didn't know how to counsel people with grief issues, and she walked out. Maybe she was right, maybe she was wrong. Even after taking a hit to the ego, you try to learn from the experience and keep going on.

I remember one session that started out in an interesting way. My client, a 6'5", three-hundred-pound man, came in for our first session. He mentioned having anxiety and a difficult time functioning in life. Five minutes into the session, he declared in a loud, nervous voice, "I think my head is going to explode!" At that moment, I didn't know if this was a medical emergency or a panic attack. I said a short prayer, sending an SOS to God, and tried to see what I could do. I began asking him to slow down his rapid breathing, gently telling him that he is in a safe place and asking him to relax various parts of his body. After a few minutes, he said he was doing a little better, but he still didn't know about his head. I asked him to stand up and told him, "We're going to take a short walk around the inside of the building." My client said, "I don't think I could stand up with my head pounding." I asked him to give it a try. He began getting out of the chair, and I was hoping he wouldn't fall over like a large tree. He got up and looked somewhat unsteady, but we began taking a few short steps out the office door. Having him focus on his breathing, we began walking down the hallway of the building. After a few laps we came back to the office, and he said he was feeling better. Thank God!

I set up all the new appointments at AC. I remember one client asked how much it cost, after telling me the reason why she wanted counseling. I replied, "It's what you can afford." The woman said she had little money and really can't afford anything. I told her, "We have to charge something because we're not getting any outside funds from the state or other resources." I asked her if five dollars a session would be all right. She said that would be fine, then there was a pause for a few seconds. "Who are you, really? Are you a part of some religious sect?" I smiled to myself and said, "No, we're just here to help out if we can." She made an appointment.

I was in the grocery store one day, talking with a friend. A lady came up to me and shook my hand and said, "Thank you for the other night." My friend looked at me with a smile and said, "I don't know how I'm supposed to take that." I hope he remembers what I do for a living.

A past client whom I hadn't seen for a few years called to ask me if I would come to her wedding. I told her I would be happy to come but asked her to think about how she would introduce me to family and friends. She told me that wouldn't be a problem because everyone already knows who I am. She also said, "You know I wouldn't be getting married without your help." After a pause, she continued, "I probably wouldn't be alive if it wasn't for you."

The years have gone by quickly at AC. Looking back at the number of people we served is humbling. We had the honor to hear many stories during those years. From 2008 through 2016, we have seen 1,516 clients. This equates to 678 women, 492 men, 224 children, and 122 couples for a total of 16,185 session hours.

I'm still running AC today, and I don't know how long it will continue. I do know that this is where God wants me to be, and I am at peace with that. I've learned so much from my clients and interns at AC that I'm truly blessed. I start each day at AC on my knees, asking God for guidance, and I end the day on my knees, giving thanks and praying for the clients I have seen. My clients have taught me many things such as compassion, patience, resilience, and love. It is a very meaningful experience to have another human being trust you with their deepest pain and fear. They trust you to understand and not to judge them. Most are stuck and want to move forward but can't. This is something I can't do all by myself; I need the Holy Spirit to enrich my sessions.

With each client who is depressed, you can use basic interventions that research has shown can reduce their depression. But it's important to make that connection with your client and use his or her life experiences, input, values, and faith, or you won't be successful. Working together on making a change is the best way.

I have learned so much from the students whom I supervise as therapists at AC. They have come in all ages, races, backgrounds, and education. The clinicians are bright and full of fight. They usually stay with me for between one and three years. Once a week we have group supervision. This is where the therapists share cases and we discuss them. A level of trust is created where the student can feel free that they won't be criticized or judged. This creates a great learning environment. I also have mental health professionals in the community come and speak to the group once a month about topics such as how to start up your own private practice, crisis intervention outreach, death and dying, domestic violence, art therapy, and many more. Such great interaction from the students and people in the field!

From all my past work experiences, I've tried to follow certain truths. The first and most important is to glorify God. As I choose a career path, is this where God wants me to be? I find a great sense of peace and joy in what I do because I'm serving God and others. There definitely have been some ups and downs; it hasn't been a straight path. Have I doubted my direction at times? Absolutely! With prayer, reflection, supportive parents, family, and friends, I got to where God was leading me. My Catholic faith has been very important to me, helping me find the right path to follow, not just in the workforce but in life in general.

My work experiences have also taught me that the people you work with are crucial for success. You can't do it alone. We all need each other. I learned that if you are going to manage others, be sure you know their job and jump in to help when needed. It is also important to know about each of them, what are their interests, goals, and dreams? I have been blessed to have many great teachers along the way, especially my dad and mom.

Behind the counter with my friend the moose,
working at a motel in downtown Las Vegas

Canterberry Coffee House 1978, on my left manager Keith
Matsumoto, busboy Albert Shidaki, and waitress Sandra Johnson

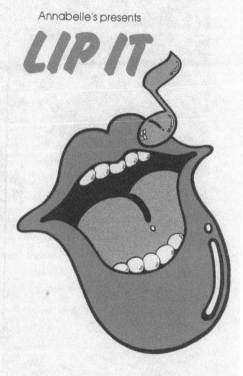

Blues Brother with the Blues Sisters

My last night at Annabelle's with Janner

Annabelle's Canoe team

2008-2016 - Affordable Counseling Interns

2

ROMANIA

"And whoever welcomes a little child like this in my name welcomes me"
(Matt. 18:5, NIV)

After getting my PhD and moving back to Seattle from California, I was staying at my parents' house, at thirty-seven years old. I spent the first two weeks, trying to find a post-doc internship so that I could get licensed to be a psychologist in the state of Washington. Sending out resumes, I had a few leads but no job yet.

The second week home, I was supposed to go out on a Friday night with some friends. For some reason, they couldn't make it, so I found myself at my parents' house, alone on a Friday night. I felt like a *big loser*. I made some popcorn and turned on the TV and *20/20* with Barbara Walters was on. One segment was on the plight of Romania's orphans. I knew after that twenty-minute piece that I was going to Romania. I knew this is what God wanted me to do. I began trying to find ways on how to do that. I only knew that Romania was in Eastern Europe, and I knew of the gymnast Nadia Comaneci. It was important that I connect with an agency to give me some credibility. Shortly after, I signed up with World Vision, a Christian relief agency. This was very exciting, because they were gathering clinicians all around the world. Then they would pair the therapists together, and they would go two by two into the cities of Romania to work in the orphanages. It reminded me of the disciples of Jesus.

A part of me still had doubts about giving up one year of my career to spend in Romania, where I couldn't get post-doc credits because it was doubtful that I could find a licensed clinical psychologist to supervise me. I could still change my mind, so about a month before I was supposed to leave, I made a pros and cons list. On the con side, I had several reasons why I shouldn't go. On the pro side, I had just one reason: That's what God wanted me to do. So I signed the papers with World Vision, even the one that stated: "If you get kidnapped by terrorists, World Vision is not responsible." I didn't show that particular paper to my mom. I said my goodbyes to family and friends. My dear friend Willie took me to the airport on a snowy Seattle January morning. On the way, I remember him saying, "Jeff, you'll come back a married man." I replied, "Willie, I have enough on my plate to think about getting married to someone in Romania." He just laughed and gave me the look: "You can think what you want, but you're coming home with a ring on your finger."

****

The following are excerpts from my journals.

It is now 11:00 p.m., I'm at Howard Johnson's, Monrovia, California, headquarters of World Vision. I will be here for one week of training. I'm ready to go. Let's get it on! I like my orientation group, who will be going to Romania, from the start. Alison (physical therapist) from London; Helen (administration) from Australia; Bev and DeWayne (administration) from World Vision; and Liviu (Romanian dentist who has been living in California with his wife, Anna). Professional and organized are two words that describe the orientation. I also like how we meet first thing in the morning for Bible reading and prayer. We have classes on the Romanian culture and language. What I am learning about some of the recent history of Romania is shocking, such as the following, excerpted from material from World Vision, 1991.

When the Communist Party came to power in Romania in 1948, the economy had been badly damaged by events of the Second World War. U.S. bombing raids had destroyed around 80 percent of the oil wells and refineries at Ploieşti which had been an important source of the country's wealth, and for a decade afterward war reparations to the USSR continued to drain resources from the economy, slowing its development.

Nicolae Ceausescu, who came to power in 1965, resolved that Romania must develop as rapidly as possible from a largely agricultural society to a modern, fully industrialized nation. To the traditional industries of oil refining, tanning, and flour milling were added new manufacturing industries, including aircraft, machinery, textiles and chemicals. To provide the workforce for his brave new industrialized state, he made it official policy from as early as 1966 that the population must increase from twenty-three million to thirty million by the year 2000. To achieve this growth, he introduced a series of laws which effectively took away from citizens their right to control the size of their families. "The fetus is the property of the entire society," he declared. "Anyone who avoids having children abandons the laws of national continuity."

Contraception and sex education were banned. In 1966, abortions were prohibited, leading to many illegal abortions, often self-induced. Hard evidence is difficult to find, but a relatively large proportion of infants appears to have been born with defects, possibly as a consequence of failed abortions. Miscarriages were subject to official investigation, and all women under forty-five years old were taken from their workplaces to clinics every one to three months for enforced medical examinations to detect signs of pregnancy. Those over twenty-five who failed to conceive—regardless of whether or not this was by choice—were liable to a "celibacy tax" of up to 10 percent of their salaries. Under these draconian edicts, the birthrate doubled.

To house the new industrial workforce, concrete blocks of flats were rapidly built, often of very low quality, and families were moved into them. Part of the new urban population was forcibly resettled from country areas. Other rural families were relocated to collective farms. Thus the existing extended family system which had acted as a supportive network was dislocated, and community ties were weakened. Feelings of responsibility to family and community were further undermined by Marxist doctrine which asserted that the individual's primary responsibility was to the State. All university courses included a compulsory element of Marxist theory, and career progress to senior positions was dependent on Party membership.

Another element tending to lead to social fragmentation was the much-feared Securitate, the secret police. They recruited informers from among ordinary citizens, and any incautious statements were liable to be reported by neighbors or workmates. According to hearsay, as many as one in four Romanians were Securitate informers; whether or not the rumor was true, it had the effect of breeding fear and suspicion, and discouraging any sort of cooperative action.

Through the 1970s, Romania achieved a high rate of economic growth, but as the world economic climate worsened at the turn of the decade, the growth rate slowed. By the early 1980s, Romania's foreign debt was among the highest in Eastern Europe. Although Western banks offered to re-schedule the debt, Ceausescu was reluctant to be dependent on foreign financial institutions, particularly if it meant Romania's human rights record coming under scrutiny. He developed an almost obsessive determination to pay off the debt at any cost, and introduced a radical tightening of the economy. The infrastructure of the country was run down—particularly the medical system, which Ceausescu saw as an unproductive consumer of resources. Although more than 60 percent of the country's land area is under cultivation, and rates of production rose with the introduction of modern agricultural methods, up to 80 percent of the output was exported to pay off the debt and food shortages became the normal state of affairs. Water and power supplies were cut back, and the people had to endure sub-zero Romanian winters with inadequate heating.

The country remained one of the poorest in Europe, with a per capita Gross National Product of U.S. $2,560 in 1988. Spending on health care, at one percent of the central government budget in 1988, was very low. Drugs and other medical supplies were in chronically short supply, and obsolete equipment could not be replaced. Information also became a scarce commodity, as in 1974 it became illegal to spend hard currency on medical journals, effectively cutting off Romanian medicine from the rest of the world, apart from a few Russian publications. Training for nurses was stopped. Doctors' salaries were extremely low—reportedly less than street sweepers'. One particularly sad consequence of poor medical practice was the infection of children with AIDS, transmitted via contaminated blood transfusions (supposed to build up malnourished, anemic infants) or through injection with dirty needles. How early such infections began or how many children were affected before the revolution is difficult to assess, but investigations after 1989 revealed some seven hundred HIV-positive children.

The combination of economic and physical hardship, social and family breakdown (divorce rates as high as 40 percent were reported) and an enforced high birth rate led to large numbers of children whose parents either did not want them or felt unable to care for them. These children became the responsibility of state-run institutions. Many mothers were forced by economic necessity to return to work after three to six months' maternity leave; 45 percent of Romania's labor force are women, leaving only a small proportion caring for children at home full time. Those who had no other childcare options left their children in a day nursery during the week. Other children whose families were in difficulty were placed in orphanages for a time until the problems could be resolved. The least fortunate were left in orphanages permanently. Romania thus achieved the dubious distinction of the highest rate of institutionalization of children in Eastern Europe at 2.4 percent; rates in Western Europe, by comparison, are normally less than 1 percent.

The Ceausescu regime viewed the abandoned kids as nothing more than a potential source of labor. At age three, those deemed "normal" were sent to preschool facilities, then to boarding schools where they learned manual skills. (Many of them, suitably dehumanized by years of institutional life, were eventually recruited into the Securitate.) But for roughly forty thousand children with physical and mental disabilities, and even such easily remedied afflictions as cleft palates or protruding ears, there was no means of escape. These supposed "irrecuperables" landed in wretched facilities that resembled nineteenth-century asylums—or even World War II concentration camps.

Then, in December 1989, following popular uprisings and the fall of governments all over Eastern Europe, troops fired on crowds in the Transylvanian town of Timisoara, unrest spread to Bucharest, and quite suddenly the Ceausescu regime was toppled. Ceausescu himself, along with his wife Elena, was tried and executed. A provisional government was formed by the National Salvation Front (NSF), an ad hoc grouping forming in the course of the uprising and led by Ion Iliescu, himself once a Communist Party Central Committee member and holder of a Party post under Ceausescu but dismissed as a potential rival.

The system for state child care—which remains essentially unchanged under the present government—is complicated, with responsibilities divided in a patchwork fashion between the Ministry of Health, the Ministry of Education and the Ministry of Labour and Social Protection. For children up to three years old, there are orphanages run by the Ministry of Health. They were designed very much on the medical model, usually with a doctor as the director. For children requiring weekday care only, the Ministry of Health provides nurseries from three months to three years. At three years old, orphanage children are screened to decide whether they will go on to a Ministry of Education institution for normal to slightly handicapped children, or to a Ministry of Labour and Social Protection-run "Camin Spital"—a home for the "irrecoverable." For a few severely handicapped children, there is a third option of Ministry of Health chronic care hospitals. Children with visual or hearing handicaps may be placed in Ministry of Education–run special schools.

The Camini Spitali were intended to cater for children and young adults between four and twenty with severe mental or physical handicaps. In practice, they have been found housing all ages up to geriatric patients, and all abilities from severe handicap to none. There are no firm statistics on the number of Spitali in existence or how many people are living in them, although there have been estimates of as many as ten thousand patients. (World Vision, 1991)

Speaking Romanian is coming slowly for me. I guess I have two left ears. The week went by fast and just like that, I was in the air on my flight to Romania. I suddenly had the feelings of apprehension. Goodbye, USA. Hello the Unknown.

Had a layover in Amsterdam. In the restroom in the airport, a musical mirror I had for the kids went off in my backpack, loudly playing "Mary Had a Little Lamb." I was praying no one would come in, and thank God no one did. I took my last hot bath at the hotel while listening to the Temptations. The time is coming near when I will get to see my kids.

Next flight was to Vienna, then to Bucharest. When I arrived in Romania, it really became a reality. *I'm here!* My two major worries did not materialize: lost luggage and no one to pick me up. My first view of Romania was at the airport, which looked like a place out of the dark ages. I feel I just jumped into a story about ancient times. The buildings are beautiful, but worn. Most of the people I have just seen are wearing furry caps because there isn't any heat in the airport.

World Vision headquarters was in Bucharest, so I was there for a week. Many meetings and getting to know the support staff. Great bunch of people. Still was anxious to get to Cluj, the city where I'll be working for a year. What calms me down is that I'm not in this alone, God will always be there. I also believe this is where I'm exactly supposed to be at this point of my life.

After sixteen hours in the air and seven hours on the train, I'm here in Cluj, the city I will make home for a year. The train station where Liviu and I arrived was dark and cold. It looked like something out of the 1940s. People were wearing long coats and fur caps; they looked so serious and I guess a little sad. On the train we met some wonderful Romanian people and when we got to Cluj, we shared a cab. Alexander, one of our train friends, invited Liviu and myself to a party at his house. Liviu declined, but I felt "as in Rome . . ." Alexander is an engineer and has a nice apartment. When we arrived at his home there were around thirty college-aged students eating, drinking and dancing to disco music. Everyone was very friendly and the food and the drinks were in abundance. So I joined them and it was fun. Cristi, a bright young man who spoke English, was my interpreter for the night. You really have to jump in and let things fly if you want to learn the culture. Not bad—one hour in Cluj and I'm already at a party. Great people. Great food and drink, a wonderful night.

Walked around the city center of Cluj with Liviu. At the heart of the town was a gothic-style church that was magnificent. I didn't know it then, but less than one year later, I would be married in that church. It appeared that Cluj was a college town, with lots of students walking around. The buildings were in the European style, small shops side by side with street vendors selling produce, flowers, and treats to eat. I must have asked Liviu a million questions about the town and language. He had a lot of patience with me.

Liviu and I were staying at the Hotel Belvedere, which was on a hill overlooking the city. We went with Barbara Bascom, MD, head of the project, to the orphanage we would be working in. She had just come in that morning from a 12-hour train ride from Budapest. Dr. Bascom was quite a remarkable lady, very business-like, goal-oriented, but at the same time with a tender and funny side. I also was told by her that I was going to be paid while I was working for World Vision. That was quite a surprise because I thought I was working for free, which was fine with me. As it turns out, the money I saved in the next two years in Romania (there really wasn't any place to spend it) came in handy for when I came back to the U.S. married and without any employment. God's plans are not always man's plans.

When we walked through the doors of the orphanage, feelings of excitement and doubt came over me. I really wanted to be there, but could I do the job? At times like these, I'm forgetting that God has sent me there and by His hand it will be all right. We met with the director of the orphanage, Dr. Maria Birtz, a lady who appeared to have gone through a lot. You could see her love for the children, and she welcomed Liviu and me to the orphanage. It also appeared that she had a cautious side to her. I had a feeling that it might take a while to gain her confidence. We met a doctor who was the head of pediatrics at the university, a very important position in the system. He told me that the physicians have little medical information from outside the country. The doctor is currently using the Nelson's 1976 pediatric book as one of his main medical resources. It's amazing what the Romanian people can do with so little. At one point when talking about the children of the orphanage, he had tears in his eyes and had to leave the room for a minute. Throughout the day, we are meeting with various staff working at the orphanage but with no involvement with the children yet. Liviu and I met with Dr. Bascom for dinner. She went over the basic objectives that she and World Vision had for the orphanage. The main goal was to get the children developmentally up to their potential as fast as possible. This orphanage had children from a few months old to five years old. At the age of five, children who were mentally and physically close to their ages' developmental ability would go to an orphanage that had a strong educational foundation. These children would have a chance to make it in life, even though they had a rocky start. The children at age five who are deemed retarded would be sent to another kind of orphanage, where they would be warehoused without any educational experiences, basically left to die.

It took five weeks of meetings at the orphanage, walking miles and miles in the cold to finally get an apartment, to get to the point that now we can start working with the children. During that time, several visitors from World Vision came to Cluj to get a look at how we were progressing. This took time because Liviu and I had to meet them at the train station and get them settled in. We also visited other orphanages outside Cluj with our guests. Another aspect that slowed things down was having several meetings with the director of the orphanage, Dr. Birtz. I guess we got off to the wrong start because World Vision sent a film crew to the Cluj Orphanage and we didn't get official permission from Dr. Birtz to film. Also another relief agency called MSF (Doctors Without Borders) had two people in the orphanage since November of 1990. I later found out that they were afraid of World Vision taking over the orphanage. All this took time to make clear, that Liviu and I just wanted to work with the children and that there wasn't any hidden agenda.

I was ready to do what I was sent for. Liviu and I met with the director and she finally gave us the go-ahead to start seeing the children. The orphanage had two buildings on the grounds. The first one was the centerpiece: a beautiful European-style building with three floors. When I saw the children on these floors, they looked like normal kids, not the ones I saw on the *20/20* TV show. The building was warm, the children looked well fed, and they were supervised. The children, ages two to four, looked developmentally close to their real age, maybe a little smaller physically. They were laughing and playing. The children also went to school onsite; I was told by Dr. Birtz the other building was also three stories tall and tucked away in the corner on the grounds. This building looked nothing like the first one. From the outside it looked run-down, with worn paint and a grey color. I asked Dr. Birtz, of the three floors, which had the most developmentally delayed children. Dr. Birtz stated Sugari II, the third floor, so I told her, "That's the floor for me." Liviu wanted to work in the main building with the more developed kids. Being separated, I would have to fend for myself with language and the staff on the floor. At this point my language skills in Romanian entailed greetings and a handful of words. With most of the staff at the orphanage not speaking English, which I liked, it made it interesting.

The day had finally come: After weeks of waiting and too many meetings, I was on my floor. The first thing I noticed was the quiet. There were twenty-five children on the floor and it was midmorning. At that time of day, I would expect to hear a lot of noise. It appeared that there weren't any children on this floor at all.

From the *People* magazine article from January 21, 1991, Barbara Bascom had a similar experience when she first met the children in other orphanages. Dr. Bascom stated, "Most eerie of all was the constant rocking by the children as they tried desperately to give themselves some sort of stimulation. . . You look into a room and they're all just swaying back and forth in unison, this absolute sea of rocking children," she reported. As I also found, Dr. Bascom said, "It was utterly silent except for the clicking of the metal cribs from the rocking back and forth."

The place was clean and warm. When I looked into the various rooms where the children were, they were all in cribs high off the floor. When I entered their living space, most of the kids began rocking back and forth, a way of comforting themselves when anxious. They all had one-piece jumpers on and most of them were wet. No sounds were made from them, just looking at me with big eyes, rocking back and forth. The children, from first glance, looked like they were from one to two years old. I later found out they were two to five years of age.

My mind began racing on all the things I had to do. I guess I should be depressed, but I'm excited at the challenge. With God's grace, the kids' needs will be met. I was told by a staff member at the orphanage that this is how it's been over the years, and you can't change anything. When I heard that, it really motivated me! The first few days, I played with the children who could tolerate it and just observed. As Dr. Bascom mentioned about the orphanages she went to, nearly every child exhibited signs of serious psychological trauma. Each floor had their own physician, but as I learned, they were never seen on the floor and left the orphanage around 2:00 p.m. The doctors only got involved if a child was sick.

During the first few weeks, being on the floor on a daily basis, I wanted to see what the nurses (infirmieres) really did on the morning and evening shifts. I worked beside them for several days to get the feel of their work. This is a general schedule of what happens on my floor, Sugari II, Monday through Friday. Sugari II has twenty-five children with the ages ranging from two to five years old.

5:50 a.m.   The 10:00 p.m. to 6:00 a.m. infirmiere was not there when I showed up. Was there a staff person on duty at all through the night? I came back a few days later around midnight to see if there was any staff in my building. The front door was locked. When I spoke to Dr. Birtz about this, she said the door was locked for safety reasons, and there was infirmieres in the building. This still didn't sit well with me, so I did a little checking into it. I found out that there was one infirmiere on for the three floors from 10:00 p.m. to 6:00 a.m. She did some random walk-throughs, then went to bed. This still wasn't acceptable, but for now, I would have to pick my battles.

6:00 a.m. Twenty out of twenty-five children asleep. Three were out of their cribs, sleeping on the floor.

6:05 a.m. Two infirmieres show up for work.

6:20 a.m. One infirmiere shows up for work.

6:30 a.m. Lights in the bedrooms are turned on. Around 50 percent of the children were asleep before the lights were turned on.

6:35 a.m. The last infirmiere shows up for work.

7:00 a.m. Two out of twenty-five children asleep. No interaction with the children yet.

7:20–7:35 a.m. "Feeding." Half of the children use bottles (the nipple of the bottle has been cut down, so the liquid passed through like a funnel except to increase the speed. Thus there is no sucking behavior, which is important for the growth of the facial muscles of the child; the other half drink from cups of a watery soup.

7:35–8:15 a.m. General clean-up and changing of the children.

8:15 a.m. "Break Time." All infirmieres on break.

8:30 a.m. Crying and screaming is heard from the different children's rooms. No reaction from the infirmieres.

8:45–9:00 a.m. Two infirmieres in playroom—two drinking coffee, one washing her hair.

9:00 a.m. Playroom (A)
Fifteen children are in room without any supervision.

A. Three children has snot coming out of their mouths to the point it is in their mouth.

B. Seven children are self-stimulating (i.e., rocking back and forth, head banging, etc.)

10:00 a.m. All four infirmieres come in to feed the children—five are given bottles, ten fed by cup. Of the ten, seven have cup held by the infirmiere. With some help, the cup-fed children can learn to feed themselves.

Feeding time takes six minutes.

11:00 a.m. Playroom B also sleep in the same room—eleven children, no supervision.

11:30 a.m. Playroom A: When I went back to check on them, five children were eating chunks of plaster they got out of an open hole in the wall. One child had vomited and was playing with it. Of course, no supervision.

11:45 a.m. Playroom A: Two infirmieres came in and took the (fifteen) children back to their beds for feeding. These children will stay in their cribs till the next morning.

Noon. Playroom B: Feeding time for seven of the eleven children, soup with little pieces of meat. No substitution is made for the four children who will not drink the soup.

12:30 p.m. Nap Time
Five out of twenty-five children asleep

1:00 p.m. Five out of twenty-five asleep

1:30 p.m. Seven out of twenty-five asleep

2:00 p.m. Eight out of twenty-five asleep

2:30 p.m. Six out of twenty-five asleep
A. One child sleeping on the floor.
Two children in one crib.

3:00 p.m. Four out of twenty-five asleep

3:30 p.m. Three out of twenty-five asleep

3:45–4:00 p.m. Feeding Time

4:05–4:45 p.m. Mass Diaper Change, took forty minutes for three infirmieres to change twenty-five children.

5:00 p.m. The cribs in Playroom B are at ground level, so the children can get out of them at will. So the children wandered around at all hours of the day and night. No supervision.

5:30 p.m. No supervision.

6:00 p.m.   No supervision.
6:30 p.m.   Only contact was a mass diaper change.
6:45 p.m.   Only contact was to feed the children.
7:00 p.m.   Lights Out. The children in Playroom/Bedroom B aren't even put to bed, the lights are just turned off.
9:00 p.m.   Twenty-two out of twenty-five asleep. One infirmiere on 10:00 p.m. to 6:00 a.m. shift. The three infirmieres on the 2:00–10:00 p.m., I believe, have gone home.
9:30 p.m.   Twenty-three out of twenty-five asleep.
10:00 p.m. twenty-four out of twenty-five asleep.

The Belgiums (MSF) told me this was the worst-run floor at the orphanage, so I'm glad I'm here. The whole section needs to be restructured and the children need to be supervised. A daily routine should be set up for the children and staff. I believe this can be accomplished but first a chain of command must be set up among the Romanians for any system to work. I know this neglect has been going on for many years here, so I will not try to change things overnight but a plan is being formed for the Sugari II.

After spending a few weeks on Sugari II, some of my initial thoughts were as follows:

1.   I believe most of the children—two to four years, do not speak at all, half cannot walk, most of the developmental delays—I believe are not due to neurological defects the children were born with. Programs need to be set up.
2.   The children should *never* be left alone.
3.   Rotation of infirmieres with the children to prevent burnout.
4.   Safety proof the playroom, begin with the radiators.
5.   Infirmieres need to constantly
       a.   walk
       b.   talk
       c.   smile
       d.   physical attention
       e.   play games (i.e., chase) with the children.

6. Small groups of children need to be formed and worked with outside the playroom. There are many places where this can happen.
7. Behavioral program setup for the children, especially for the ones who show autistic and self-destructive behavior.
8. Organize and restructure Sugari II with the help/input of the infirmieres/MDs/director.
9. Encourage the instruction of daily living skills to the children that are developmentally ready:
    a. eating on one's own
    b. toilet training
    c. dressing oneself
    d. washing hands/ brushing teeth

I would begin testing the children on my floor, then move on to other floors in the orphanage. I brought over the Bayley Infant Development test to use with each of the children. I had been working with a Romanian psychologist, who had been helping me getting the Bayley translated into Romanian, so other groups can use it. I did not have the original Bayley testing kit but used similar objects and toys.

After spending a week on the floor, I knew I needed extra help to get these kiddos up to speed. I offered my teaching services at the University of Cluj with the intention to get some students to volunteer at the orphanage. They were happy to have me teach a course of psychology because it was never taught under the rule of former director, Nicolae Ceausescu. It's been over twenty-five years since psychology has been taught in Romania.

On February 26, 1991, I began teaching a child psychology class to forty students with a translator. Some of the general areas that would be presented were biological bases of development, prenatal development, infancy and growth, emotional and language development. With all these topics, I would try to use a lot of examples from the orphanage. Fourteen of the students were willing to volunteer, two days a week, four hours a day. I discussed this with the director and she would not give me her approval even to a small group of five students. I told Dr. Birtz I would always be at the orphanage when the students were there, and I would directly supervise them. At last, she did grant approval for the students to visit the orphanage. It appears there has been a problem in the past with volunteers.

In March of 1991, I tested the twenty-five children on my floor, Sugari II, with the Bayley Infant Development test. All the children were significantly below their age level on mental and motor abilities. I also gave the Bayley's to the first floor, the "Parter," where the children were supposed to be more developed. As a group, they tested higher but still below their age level. The Parter also had a group of infants, which were too young to test. The second floor, Sugari I, was run by MSF, and they didn't request testing.

After the assessment of the children on my floor, I picked out seven of the least developed out of the twenty-five children. These children probably had some severe neurological damage, but you didn't know for sure because they were never given a chance to thrive. I would see these kiddos three times a week individually for an hour. They were seen for between sixteen and eighteen months.

The children I saw in individual sessions were as follows:

	Chronological Age		Mental Age	Motor Age
	Year	Months		
Woarda	7	0	4 months	3 months
Sabastian	2	9	4 months	8 months
Csilla	2	11	5 months	8 months
Melinda	4	8	4 months	11 months
Marcel	5	0	1 year	1 ½ years
Roxana	3	4	9 months	9 months
Dememy	2	11	4 months	10 months

The other children, I would put in small groups, depending on their ability. The groups were as follows: The Walkers, The Crawlers, The Movers, and The Girls. These groups met twice a week. Some of the activities we did were the following: Water Play—filled a plastic tub full of water and have the children experience the water with their hands, cups, floating toys, etc. They would also experience flowers, grass, dirt, or seeds in a plastic tub to have the children feel and smell the different items. We also used Play-Doh and blowing up balloons and playing with them. The most popular group activity was Water Play, where eventually we all got soaked.

From my clinical journal, here are some observations I had through the months.

Roxana

Birthday 11/17/87. Entry date 10/3/88. Mother: Single. Father: Unknown.

Occupation: None. Reason for Roxana being brought to the orphanage: Mother lives alone with five children.

General observations of Roxana in early March of 1991:

Social Interaction:
1. She is responsive to attention, can pick out certain caregivers over others, can differentiate.
2. Can be overstimulated easily and then will go into protective position, on her back, with her hands up.
3. Minimal physical interaction with her peers but seems interested on what is going on around her.

Communication:
1. Can laugh, imitate sounds, some nonsensical words/ sounds.

Motor Development:
1. Can sit up, can stand, but will only stand up when she wants to. When you try to have her walk, she will tuck her legs up underneath her.
2. Stereotypical "hand waving gestures," will stare at her hands.

3. When she feels threatened, will lay on her back and use her legs as weapons.

Testing on the Bayley's in March of 1991 for Roxana shows a chronological age of three years and four months, mental age of eight months, and motor age of eight months.

Some of the highlight sessions of working with her from 3/5/91 to 8/12/92:

3/5: First individual session—have played with her in a group setting the last two weeks. Carried her down the hall to my office (she couldn't walk). Stayed there briefly and went back to the playroom.

3/11: When given a toy by me or if she picks one up, she would throw it away.

3/12: Playroom observation: Played chase with the children who could walk, she joined the game, moving by sitting on her bottom. Can she crawl?

3/14: "Roxana Walked Today."

When I came into the playroom, an infirmiere was holding her hands, and she was standing up. I then proceeded to walk her around the playroom and down the hall. Roxana walked stiff legged, but she walked holding one or both of my hands. At the end of session, she grabbed onto a standing bar in my room, got on her feet. It seemed she enjoyed her newfound success.

3/19: "Roxana Walked on Her Own."

She could take around ten steps without any assistance. Roxana did a lot of walking up/down the hall tonight, with and without help.

4/8: Was told by the infirmiere that Roxana ate/drank very little the last two days. They asked for my help to feed her today. At the start, she was scared and moved away from the cup. When I got behind her and held her, she drank two cups of a milky substance. Goal: To monitor and increase her eating.

4/12: "First Day Roxana Engaged in Play."

We rolled a small ball back and forth for five minutes. She rolled the ball in my direction and appeared to like the interaction.

4/19: Consult with Gail, occupational therapist (OT), who was visiting from California. To hold Roxana on the hips from the back when walking instead of pulling her along by her hands.

4/23: Box riding: Sat in a cardboard box, and I pushed her up and down the hallway. Roxana laughed loudly. She stayed in the box throughout the session, did not try to get out.

5/29: Roxana is walking more but limited vocalizations and no words. We can interact in mutual play for up to five minutes, then she breaks it off.

6/24: Took Roxana outside of the front entrance of her building. Could do some walking but overall was overstimulated—could stay outside for seven minutes. Back in my office, she calmed down quickly.

6/26: Said, "Da" ("yes") three times and initiated hand play with me.

7/2: Tried a new technique with Roxana today. In the past, it seems at the beginning of session, she is overwhelmed by being in my office. And it takes between ten and fifteen minutes before she interacts with me. Some days, she wouldn't interact at all. This time I gave her more space by sitting outside my office with the door open. Roxana had her choice to interact with me or go back into the safety of the office. Some of my observations:

1. Roxana vocalized much more, walked in and out of the office and interacted with me at the beginning of session (i.e., we threw a plastic ring back and forth).
2. This technique gives her more control of her environment, thus it appears she is more open.
3. *Da Da*—six times.
4. Would not leave the office when the session ended, had to carry her out and she squirming all the way.

7/9: This session should be called "The Day Roxana Destroyed My Office."

She explored the office from top to bottom. She was grabbing things off my desk, playing with all the toys, which she spread out all over the floor, knocked over a chair, and knocked over a glass, which broke on the floor (a good sign of her improvement). Focused on her play and not distracted by outside noises as in the past. Very upset when she was brought back to her unit, began hitting her head against the wall. Took her a while to calm down. Through the months working with Roxana, I learned to be more passive and let her go at her speed.

7/16: "The Day Roxana Made It to the Park."

There is a grassy area with trees right on the grounds of the orphanage. The farthest she has made it outside her building was just a few steps a month ago. To my surprise, once I put her on the grass, she twirled around on her bottom. She laughed and pulled up the grass and threw it. What joy! Roxana even walked around. The only thing that seemed to scare her was the sounds of trucks nearby.

8/8: Spent most of session in the park, really enjoyed riding the swing. She let out a big burst of laughter. In the grass, she wasn't as verbal. Did throw some grass around.

8/23: Park observations: Roxana went down the seven-foot slide several times. She gives a happy scream when sliding down, can get off by herself, walk around to the steps, needs help up the steps but can slide down on her own. It was hard to have Roxana leave the park today. She kept running back to the slide (a very good sign).

10/28: Went visiting other floors, could walk down two flights of stairs. Roxana had one arm raised over her head while meeting new people. Visited the playroom on the first floor, which had five children playing, all around Roxana's age. She appeared frightened in this new environment and stayed close to me.

11/11: Said "Mama"! ("mother")!

12/13: Session in office. Roxana was very active. She interacted with me in many ways (i.e., game of chase, banging objects together). She appeared alert and wanted to be near me. Roxana cried when I brought her back to the playroom.

2/18: Roxana put on an adult-size jacket, gloves, hat, and played dress-up for the first time. Made some Da Da sounds.

3/3: When a stranger came into my office today, Roxana came over and sat on my lap. When the person left, she got off me and went on playing. Would not engage in ball throwing at first but, after a while, could roll the ball back to me three times.

3/23: Roxana said the word "Apa" ("water") for a few times at the beginning of session, a little later, she said "Apa" again and pointed to the tub where I put water in.

4/3: Roxana beginning to say some sounds that resemble words. Waved goodbye and said something that sounded like "Tai Tai" ("goodbye.")

5/3: Session in office, could put 60 percent of the shapes into the holes. Beginning to "baby talk" in her play.

5/18: Picture cards. Roxana could repeat three words from the cards, somewhat clearly. She then threw most of the cards on the floor and would not concentrate on the task. Roxana is babbling more and the sounds are sounding closer to words.

5/19: Took Roxana outside, explored the plants, trees, watched the cars. Also sat on a bench and watched people go by.

6/2: Dr. Gardner, a psychiatrist from England, visited the orphanage. During lunch, she spoke about a holding technique used especially for autistic children. You get on the floor, have the child sit behind your outstretched legs with its back pressing on your chest (i.e., like a basket hold for out-of-control small children). You start out for two minutes and gradually increase the time. The hope is that the child will be more comfortable with human contact.

Had five sessions using the technique with Roxana. Most of the time she struggled and cried out. This technique was hard on me emotionally because I knew she didn't like it. In the past fifteen months, working with Roxana, we had limited physical contact. This new method must have seemed strange and frightening to her. Dr. Gardner reports there has been some great breakthroughs using this technique. I was torn on what to do.

6/19: Two infirmieres reported in the last two weeks, Roxana has been pulling out her hair. By closer look, I could see missing spots on her head. It seemed Roxana began pulling her hair out right around the same time I started using the new technique. Later in the day, when I came into the playroom, she ran from me.

6/22: Still looking for a breakthrough with the holding method but after the session had the same results, Roxana being afraid of me and not liking the direct contact.

6/24: Will discontinue this method because it's causing her much stress and she has regressed from the things she has learned. Did not use holding method during this session but she is very afraid of me, cried a lot, wanted to leave my office, and stood by the door.

6/25: Stayed away from Roxana, gave her space in the office. At times, she was her old self, laughing and coming over to me. But at other times still fearful.

6/30: Roxana showed "concern" about me being in pain when she threw a chair down that hit my knee. Roxana appeared comfortable with me, she even came over and sat on my lap for a few seconds.

8/12: After about eighteen months, I decided to stop seeing Roxana in individual sessions. Through the last two months, she came back to the same level before the holding technique. Overall, limited interaction with others and few vocalizations/words.

Roxana, most of time when I saw her in park, tended to be by herself. I feel to some degree the holding technique slowed down her progress, and I wished I hadn't done it. Roxana is still being seen in group and in the classroom. We try to keep most of the kids as active as possible. I will continue to see Roxana in her various settings and always keep praying for her.

The other child I would like to highlight of the seven children I saw in individual therapy is Woarda.

Woarda

Birthday 3/4/84. Entry date 3/31/84. Reason for Woarda being brought to the orphanage: Mother is 17 years old, not married, unemployed. Father does not recognize Woarda as his child.

Premature with 2.6 kgs. Birthweight and hepatitis was reported. Four days after birth, jaundice was diagnosed.

10/84: Retarded psychomotor due to her many illnesses and poor stimulation.

3/85: Poor muscle development and brain development.

1/86: Does not respond to toys or stimulation.

Reports dated till 6/90 show no progress and mental retardation.

I tested Woarda with the Bayley's in March of 1991, which showed a chronological age of seven years and one month, mental age of four months, motor age of two months and fifteen days. Even though I knew she was extremely below her age, those numbers on the Bayley's still were shocking. My attitude was "With God's help, let's roll up our sleeves and see what we could do."

I was told that Woarda never left her crib and always stayed on her side. She was bottle fed, seldom made any sounds, and has never spoken a word. The only time she came in contact with a caregiver was when she was fed and changed in her crib.

3/5: Morning. She laid on her side throughout the session, with hands over her head. It appears that this is a natural position for her. Woarda withdrew from my touch and was afraid of the contact. Did make some eye contact. Goal: to have Woarda be comfortable with me. Treatment plan: Small amount of physical contact, don't want to overstimulate.

Afternoon. She made eye contact, some light physical contact. When she began to cry, I stopped. She did grab my finger two times.

3/11: First time in my office, did not cry.

1. Still on right side, arms covering both ears, legs tucked (i.e., fetal position).
2. Few times raised head to look around.
3. Minimal eye contact.
4. Reached out twice for a toy.

Treatment Plan:

1. Physical contact, rubbing her back, legs, and side.
2. To gently move her into different positions (she cried when she was put halfway on her back).
3. To slowly get her involved with her environment outside her crib.

3/12: Playroom observation:

In the corner by herself. Constant rocking back and forth. When I rubbed her back, she cried.

3/13: Woarda showed a lot of emotion today, laughed when touched, could roll her on back. She reached out and touched my face and hands. I carried her up and down the hall without any crying. Minimal eye contact but didn't have that distant stare.

3/15: Carried Woarda up and down the hall. She was very curious of her surroundings. Intervention in office: Put Woarda on a soft mat and because she is always on her side, try to roll her on her back and other side. At first she resisted but at the end of session, could lay on her back without crying.

4/3: Set Woarda on my lap facing me. She was in a sitting position and, for the first five minutes, appeared very anxious. She had both arms over her head and did not make any eye contact. Second five minutes, one arm down, played with my hand. Third five minutes, both arms down, one hand holding my hand, the other hand playing with my watch.

4/8: Woarda hit the keys of a toy piano by herself. Also could be in a sitting position with slight support for ten minutes.

4/10: When I came to get her from her crib, she was sitting up. *Wow!* It appears she is getting used to her expanded world. She is looking around more in the playroom or when I take her to different places on her floor.

4/15: Consultation with Gail Hearder, visiting occupational therapist (OT) from the USA. Some of her recommendations were:

1. Gentle rotation of Woarda's arms, legs, and feet.
2. Try to get her on her stomach as much as possible.
3. When using the ball, have her reach out for it.

4/18: Used the information from the consult with Gail to add on to the things we are already doing. Lots of gentle manipulations of her arms and legs; she even laughed and smiled. She wasn't anxious when I rolled her from side to side. It seems being on her stomach is still uncomfortable for her. Her vocalizations have increased from none at all to laughing and making a popping sound with her lips.

4/25: The day Woarda said, "Mama"!

It's amazing but true. My friend Cristi heard her say "Mama" first, when he shouted for me to come quick. I heard Woarda say "Mama." I can't believe it from random babbling to saying a word. What a joy!

6/6: First time I took Woarda outside the building. She held on tight but did not cry. She was more comfortable in the shade, it seemed that the sun bothered her eyes. Laughing, making sounds while on my lap.

6/21: Went to the park with Woarda. She was laughing and making a lot of sounds. She even rode the merry-go-round play equipment for five minutes by herself.

6/25: Said "Mama" two times today.

7/9: Observation: Woarda was sleeping on her stomach, not on her side.

9/23: Most of our sessions through the summer were in the park. She appeared mostly happy, alert, and at times laughed. Kept working on moving and positioning her body in different positions. She would let out a cry when she didn't like something.

12/6: Alert, the best I have seen her. Woarda appeared more aware of her surroundings and her attention more focused. She is sitting much better and is more active/interested in objects.

12/31: Woarda, on one occasion, responded to my voice and followed the directions. She was in a sitting position and began sliding down to be on her side. When I said "no-no," she stopped and sat back up. This is the first time Woarda has responded to my words. She was happy and active and could play with objects in both hands.

2/3: Observation: Still laying on her side in the playroom, needs to be sitting in car seat (spoke with the caregivers, they will begin right away).

3/7: A rash/bruise like marks on her arms and some on her back. I spoke with Dr. Skana, and she will check it out and would get back to me.

3/11: Woarda went to the hospital.

3/26: Came back today from the hospital. She had a tube in her nose because she wouldn't eat there. Tried to give her a bottle when she arrived back. Refused with lots of crying. She could sit in her car seat and play with two objects. I carried her around the floor to let her know that she is back home. Ate in the evening and had two bottles in the morning.

4/6: Woarda happy affect when I brought her to the office. Would not drink her bottle at noon. Massage and rolling, which she appeared to enjoy.

4/23: Woarda played with a pencil and leaned over to me for some physical contact. Massage and played with different objects. Happy and laughed a lot during the session. Good eye contact.

4/25: When I arrived on Saturday for a quick check-in with Cristi, I got a very sad shock. Woarda had died in the early morning. At this point, we don't know why. When I asked the staff where Woarda was, they said they put her in a box, and she is out on the balcony. Because she died on the weekend, she wouldn't be moved till Monday and taken down to the morgue to be examined and put to rest. I was angry! This was unacceptable. She can't just be left there like a sack of garbage. I'm glad Cristi was there to calm me down because I would have probably said some things in Romanian and English that I would later regret. It wasn't anyone's fault. I believe her body just gave out. I'm glad she had some moments of happiness along the way. Now what to do with Woarda? I decided to take Woarda to the morgue today. We wrapped Woarda in bed sheets, called a taxi, and waited outside the orphanage to get picked up. I guess it looked like I was holding a bag of laundry. The taxi driver didn't make any comment. Cristi and I said a prayer for Woarda and left her at the morgue. The orphanage doctor will call on Monday to make the arrangements. Woarda is not laying on her side anymore but is totally free, in a place where she is loved all the time. I'll miss her lopsided smile and laugh. God bless you, little one!

4/30: They found fluid in the back of Woarda's head.

During my two years at the orphanage, besides seeing children in individual sessions, I saw the rest of the children in small groups.

I had a plastic tub which I brought out during a lot of our groups. I filled it with all sorts of things so the children can experience their different senses. Water play in the tub was one of the kids' favorites. I filled the tub halfway and put different objects inside. During other groups I put dirt, flowers, and gravel in the tub. They enjoyed these sensations but not as much as playing in the water. Play-Doh Time, Drawing, Big Yellow Ball, and whatever I could throw into the mix for our little groups. An educator from the church took over the group after the first five months, which freed me up to do other things. They still would have various play activities, but the focus would be on the Romanian language and general education.

After three months being on my floor, there was new life, a sense of kids being kids, getting into anything they can, being curious, making noise, talking and much more. They were all out of their cribs during the day. There was now a schedule for the day for the children. It runs smoothly when I was there, but the trick was to have it followed when I'm not there. I had been meeting with the infirmieres and the physician in charge to get their input. For the most part, they had not suggested a lot and feel they can follow the program. The infirmieres reported they were already doing these things, which was true, but they were not consistent and didn't involve all the children on the floor. The doctor or myself had to be there in the morning to get the ball rolling. The idea was to try to empower the infirmieres. Some ways I had tried to do this with the new program were to (a) ask for feedback, take their comments and suggestions as being valid and important, (b) having a set time frame for daily events. This way the infirmieres know what was expected of them and they didn't need someone else to tell them what to do. The fun had just begun. I expected the infirmieres to test the program by not following through on some of the objectives. I would be there during important periods of the day to see that the program was being followed. Putting structure in the children's day with various activities will help them developmentally. To have the infirmieres follow the system, they had to believe in the system.

But more important than a system for the children was that the staff believe in the children they take care of. When I started on

Sugari II, the general attitude of the doctors and infirmieres were that the kids on my floor were subhuman. They were just something you had to change its diaper and feed a few times during the day. They weren't seen as children. Several of the staff had children themselves, and naturally they treated their own children differently. That's what I wanted them to do: treat the orphanage children as their own. All the daily plans, education, and structure could not achieve that. I didn't have the answer and all my motivational talk through the early months wasn't taking hold. The answer came a few months into the new program. The children held the key to changing the staff's general attitude about them. With more stimulation and contact with adults, they began to form their own identities. They gave back to the staff by smiling back to them and not having a blank stare. They began to say words and interact with the staff. They began to be more independent by taking care of their own needs. They began to feed themselves and go to the toilet (there are stories to be told later). Most of the staff began calling them by their names. The children turned the program around.

I had the opportunity to work with several groups from other countries that wanted to help out at the orphanage. Ruud Tropman and his group from Holland came over to help in July of 1991 and came back again in the summer of 1992. Ruud was a bigger-than-life character with a booming voice and a smile on his face. He brought over a group of around twenty young adults each visit, who were very excited to help. They brought in a lot of needed things that was wanted by the orphanage staff. Because Holland was located near Romania, they could drive the supplies in. Ruud and group brought in thirty lower-level kid beds, so those children wouldn't be trapped in their cribs anymore. Each child would have a place to put their clothes (there was a need now for shoes, coats because the child was going outside). It was such a joy to see the nasty, paint-chipped cribs be taken out. Holland group also did various jobs around the orphanage and painted several rooms and hallways with brighter colors, not like the institutionalized color of gray that was the dominant color at the orphanage. They were such a blessing with all they did around the orphanage. The time and money spent by them were wonderful gifts they gave to the children. Their uplifting attitude spread around the orphanage to us all as a beacon of hope.

On July 13, the youth group (fourteen) from La Canada Presbyterian Church, Pasadena, California, arrived at the orphanage. Their two weeks were spend doing a lot of back-breaking work which included digging out large sections of ground for the new play equipment, which was worth $40,000 and had to be constructed. The adult group from various Presbyterian churches in the U.S. arrived on July 24. This group of eighteen put in the play equipment, painted windows and cribs. Both groups were hard working and independent. When the play equipment was all put up, it was a beautiful sight to see. Sand was put on the ground where the play equipment was so to soften the impact of the children when they fell down. Slides and climbing equipment, rope climb, lots of cool things to give the children a great physical workout. All the floors of the orphanage used the play equipment on a daily basis. To hear the kids laughing, yelling, and just being kids was a moment I'll always remember.

On August 27, 1991, six wonderful people from England arrived at the orphanage to paint murals. They just showed up one day and told what they would like to offer to the orphanage. Wow! I never turn down generous folks so they started the next day. They stayed for eight days. They painted characters on my section and the director's section (politically I believe a good move). The paintings fit in well with the newly painted walls that the Holland group just completed. When you come up the stairs to my section, the first thing you'll see is a wacky rabbit bidding you welcome. To the left of the stairs, the artist painted a huge Noah's ark with all sorts of animals coming out and running down the hall. With all the colorful characters in the hallway, playroom and bedrooms, it now looks like a floor for children. This was a hard-working group of folks putting in ten-hour days. They will long be remembered.

Andy Whitelock was a huge blessing when he came to work at the orphanage. He was a pre-med student from La Canada Church, giving a year of his life to try to make things better for the children of Romania. Andy worked on the floor below my floor, Sugari Parte. He spent a lot of time building rapport with the staff and getting to know how the section ran. He fit right in because he was so genuine and energetic the women staff on his floor really liked him. Did I mention he was tall and good looking? A daily living program for the children was implemented as Andy got more comfortable with the children and staff.

Amy Semple from the U.S. came to work at the orphanage for several months. Amy was another big blessing especially with her energetic personality. It was great to have a fresh pair of eyes to ask questions and make comments on the running of the orphanage. She would be working with the infants. One thing I noticed when I was first on the infant floor was the silence. Once in a while I would hear a cry out but for the most part it was quiet and this was in the middle of the day. I learned when the infants first came to the orphanage, they cried out like normal babies. They learned in a short period of time it didn't matter, no one would come to meet their needs. They would be fed and changed on a set schedule. After a short period of time, they gave up. This sense of hopelessness left untreated would stunt their emotional and physical growth. With Amy on the floor and having some extra pair of hands, the deadly silence was gone. The staff's attitude with time changed, and they fed off the energy from Amy and Andy. Was it difficult at times to change an underpaid, lethargic, and disinterested staff? Of course, there were days when the light at the end of the tunnel was flickering. Changing the staff's feelings toward the children and us changing and expanding our mindset toward the staff was an ever-developing process. With God's grace, great strides were made. With daily prayer and reflection, it set the stage for the day. We weren't doing our work, we were doing God's work. A therapist I worked with in the U.S. mentioned this saying, which I have always remembered: "God's Will, God's Bill." God will provide! That's what kept us going.

Looking at the different experiences I had through the two years at Romania, there are simply too many to recount. Some of the highlights are as follows.

Kids Storm the Park

I was told by the director of the orphanage that in her ten years at the orphanage, she has never seen any of the children on my floor go to the park. Well, she can't say that any longer. By gradually shaping their behavior to get them used to being outside, five children from my floor were going to the park on a regular basis. This increased to most of the children of my floor in a few months. You had to go at the child's speed, if you push too much they could be traumatized. It's a real joy to see these little ones running around and exploring every little twig and piece of grass.

Christmas Comes to the Orphanage

I was told by the staff that they really didn't have a Christmas celebration on any of the floors. Well, that had to change. So with a bit of help from Cristi, Andy, Donal, and others, we planned, organized, and ran a Christmas party for the whole orphanage. Each floor had their own live Christmas tree. We even had a tree-decorating contest. Santa (Monica's dad) came to the orphanage as big as life. I think most of the children didn't know who he was and were somewhat set back at first. When Santa brought a toy for each child, they started to loosen up. Santa also passed out eighty bags of coffee to the staff members. We had music and various singing and dancing groups of children from the various floor. Overall I don't know how much the children comprehended the Christmas program but you did see several smiles and looks of amazement. I believe the part the children liked best of the whole day was when they got out of their new clothes and did some serious playing with the new toys. The director, Dr. Birtz, seemed pleased and the mayor gave a thank-you speech to the World Vision staff. One infirmiere stated it was the best Christmas she had seen in her twenty-eight years working at the orphanage.

Kids Hit the Snow!

On December 26, fourteen children from my floor, all bundled up in their winter suits (compliments of La Canada Church), made it out in the snow for the first time in their lives. All the children but one stayed outside and played with this new substance called snow. They were cautious at first but opened up soon to eating it and having a mini snowball fight. We hired two caregivers to bring out the children on a daily basis. Sun, rain, and now even snow—the children will be outside on a regular basis. I like to think of these two caregivers as the children's outside teachers.

I hired a retired schoolteacher from the local church. Mrs. Jenny was a fireball during my interview with her. Full of energy and had a set plan to teach her new students. I liked her a lot! One of her primary goals was language development. She now runs several small groups in a newly created classroom. She has done a wonderful job with the children. A handful of the students are beginning to say some words (water, hello, food, music, and Jeff). As the weeks went by, the children were beginning to communicate their needs. Another improvement was socialization skills. In the playroom you can now see children playing with each other. In the past it was "every man for himself," with lots of parallel play (being side by side but not interacting with one another). In the playroom, now you can see the children playing with each other. You can pick out the good buddies of some of the kids.

Within one year entering the old building on the side of the main showcase building, there are a total of fourteen caregivers now working on two floors with MSF working on another floor. The women are all from the local churches. Three of the helpers are teachers who have had many years of experience. The educators run classes daily with six to eight children per group. A total of thirty-two children now go to a structured teaching program. Some of the skills taught range from brushing teeth to language development. A weekly meeting is held with the caregivers to discuss needs.

Most of the children now eat at tables in a room I set up as a dining room. At the beginning the kids sure made a big mess eating their soup with a spoon. Some children needed one on one attention. Several infirmieres mentioned that this way of feeding the children was a lot of work and just giving them bottles was a lot easier. Teaching the children to feed themselves in the long run would be even easier than bottles. Many of the orphanage staff had children of their own. I asked to remember the feeding progression of their children. The eating program with a lot of clean-up at the beginning soon became the norm on the floor. Extra staff from the churches was added to help with the feeding and not to put a heavy load on the infirmieres. It's easy at times to be pushy and "Why aren't the staff doing this and that?" Unless you have the patience, give extra help, and worked right along with the staff, any program you set up is doomed to fail. You can have all the plastic plates, bibs, spoons, etc., but if you can't motivate the staff to carry it out, these items will just gather dust.

Another program I implemented around the same time the kids were learning to feed themselves was the potty program. The children were conditioned to walk down the hall to the bathroom area right after they ate. I had gotten twelve plastic portable potties for the children to train on. The potty program took two months to iron out the rough spots and to have the infirmieres follow it on a regular basis. As more and more children mastered the concept it became less work for the staff; thus they would then reinforce it. Also added a hand-washing routine after they used the potty. You should have seen the look of pride and amazement after the children did their business in the plastic potties and took their potty to dump in the toilet. They were learning to be more and more independent. What a blessing because to some degree they are shaping their future.

The more the children progressed, the more hands were needed. By April of 1992, there were seventeen caregivers and four educators (all Romanian) working with a total of seventy-seven children. These World Vision–funded helpers were now on four of the seven sections at the orphanage. Programs included outdoor activities, teaching in a classroom setting, videos, playroom structure, games, motor development, and lots of love. A morning and afternoon meeting was held each week with the caregivers and educators. I meet with each educator once a week to discuss individual children and program development. In May, four more caregivers were hired, and their responsibility would be taking the children outside seven days a week. The children were getting bigger and bigger, and they need a place to roam.

Miracle on the third Floor

Claudia, a five-year-old developmentally delayed girl, fell out a three-story window and survived with minor injuries. Claudia landed on a big bag of bird poop which was left right below the window. The doctor in charge had to give her CPR because she had stopped breathing. Claudia was in the hospital for a short stay. After the shock died down and thanking God for watching out for Claudia, we needed to find out what happened so we wouldn't have any more kids flying out the window. It was found that the bathroom window was left open where the children use the potties. Claudia finished her meal early and then went directly to the potties unescorted. A screen on the window was put on and a better plan of supervision was later worked out.

Summer of '92, language was really becoming a major part of a lot of the children on my section. The most used words, to no surprise, were the ones that got the children's needs met ("I want this," "Give me that," "Do this for me"). The children were beginning to put the words in sentences and carry on mini conversations with the staff. By asking the staff different questions, it reinforces the caregivers to talk back to the children. In the eyes of the caregivers, the children were becoming more human with their own personalities, not just something you had to feed and change. It was really great to hear some of the more developed children speaking with each other. It was fun to eavesdrop on them when they were supposed to be sleeping and hear their little conversations.

As the children grew, so did the program that the kids followed. It appeared the little ones were ready for change and growth, but the adults took a little longer. For example, we received some beautiful handmade cloth blankets, perfect for each child to sleep with. Each blanket was different so we had the children pick out their favorite one, then put their name on it. It took several times to get the point across to the staff, that even though the room was warm and the blanket wasn't needed to protect them from the cold, it was still important for the child to have. The blanket was the first thing in the children's life that was truly theirs. It gave a sense of security like that of a mother. I believe the staff began to understand that a piece of cloth could be much more to a child than they could imagine. I needed to keep working on my frustration with the staff and understand with God's grace and patience from above, thy will be done.

Children on the Move

In October of 1992, eight children had left my floor (Sugari II) either to go to another section in the orphanage or to a new orphanage. This many children leaving was unusual for the staff, and their emotions ran high. Some of the staff had tears in their eyes while others showed their emotions through anger towards the administration. For me, when the little ones left, it was a sad day because I'll miss them very much, but also a happy day because the children are going to more advanced sections.

The first Bible class for the orphanage children was held on Nov. 23, 1992. Two Romanian ladies conducted the class of eight children. They will be teaching one afternoon a week beginning with my section, then moving on to other sections in the future. The women had begun working with my educator by giving her lesson plans and supplies regarding the Bible. The educator was very excited about teaching the children about God, that she would spend ten minutes each day on this important subject. This plan to have lesson plans about God moved to the other floors. This was possible because the director of the orphanage was 100 percent behind it. This was a dream of Andy Whitelock (intern from California who stayed a year), in which he put a lot of time and energy in getting everyone together. Thanks to Andy, these wonderful ladies, and the director's support, these Bible classes are now a reality.

January 1993, after two years working with these little ones, it was time to say goodbye. Watching them grow, hearing their first words, the first step, seeing the light in their eyes (there was someone at home), acting like normal kids had been so rewarding! *You've come a long way, baby! You have changed the hearts of many of the staff, which appeared cold at the start.* With joy came sadness; seeing a few of the children die was heartbreaking. Many types of emotions would be going through me when I walked out that door for the last time. It would probably be one of the most difficult things I would ever have to do. It was reassuring to know that the children would always be in God's big hands. There were now programs/caregivers to carry on with the work. Mrs. David would be responsible for the running of the twenty-five caregiver program of Romanian women getting paid by World Vision. Some of her duties would be to calculate the monthly caregiver payroll, introduce educational development, take charge of disciplinary matters, and work closely with the orphanage director. Mrs. David's twenty-six years' experience of working with children and being a supervisor would really be a blessing to the caregiver program. The whole philosophy of World Vision coming to the orphanage was to hand it back to the Romanians after giving them resources and expertise in some areas. This took time, but I think two years was a good time frame because change is not easy. The Romanian people are very resilient throughout their history. With World Vision funding some extra caregivers and setting up some structure on the floors, the "show will go on." Goodbye, little ones, you will always be with me.

To end this chapter on my experiences in Romania, I would like to write about a little girl who changed a lot of lives, including myself and my wife Monica. Caterina was born in February 21, 1989 and entered the Cluj Orphanage in May of 1990. There isn't any reported information on Caterina's mother and father. The records show little developmental history on Caterina. I began working on her floor when she was two years old. She was just one of many kids on the floor and not one of the children I saw individually. I remember that she was passive and withdrawn when I first encountered her. She used to stand in her bed and rock back and forth, especially if someone walked into her room. This was a way of soothing herself when she got anxious. With a steady flow of healthy stimulation (i.e., talking with her, getting her out of her bed, playing with various toys, and interacting with others), Caterina made steady progress. Given the opportunity, Caterina reached various developmental milestones ahead of most children on her floor. She walked alone at two and a half years, could say a few words at two years and ten months, eat solid foods by herself at two years and seven months, used the potty at three years old, dressed/undressed (60 percent) at three years and two months. Regarding social interactions, Caterina needed to check out the situation or person before committing herself. She is friendly with her peers but not to the point of being taken advantage of. Caterina would scream and throw a punch if another child tries to take away a toy from her. She has a best friend named Stella, who is at Caterina's developmental level. They like to sit together when they eat and do other activities together.

On the Bayley Scale of Infant Development, Caterina had the following scores:

Mental Age on 3/91	Mental Age on 9/91	Mental Age on 3/92
three months	fourteen months	twenty months
Motor Age on 3/91	Motor Age on 9/91	Motor Age on 3/92
eight months	sixteen months	twenty-five months

The results indicate steady progress. I remember in a report about Caterina, I wrote, "Given the chance to grow up with appropriate stimulation, Caterina can catch up developmentally to her chronological age. In a normal environment, after some adjustment problems, Caterina should do fine." The question was with Caterina and the other children on my floor, would they have enough time to achieve these developmental milestones? A decision would be made when the children reached five years old, what type of orphanage they would go to next.

I thought the story ended there, but it just got started. In the summer of 1991, a wonderful couple from Malibu, California, Doug and Lisee, came to visit the orphanage with other people from World Vision. A district director for World Vision, Doug began working to coordinate churches, individuals, corporations, and foundations to assist World Vision in supplying medical and educational aid to the orphanage. The La Canada Presbyterian Church had made donations and in May of 1991 sent a survey team to Cluj to see what their money had accomplished. Doug represented World Vision on taking the team over. One of the church members felt so strongly that it would be a life-changing experience that Doug's wife Lisee should go along and paid her way.

World Vision was not encouraging adoptions but was working to reestablish children within Romanian society. Doug and Lisee were not considering adoption. Lisee remembered her first encounter with Caterina. "We were there two weeks, but I didn't see Caterina until the second to last day… She was in a group of kids crawling on the floor. My attention was drawn to her because she reminded me of a friend's child. I picked Caterina up and she sat with me. I started to sing and she started humming with me. I was so taken with her, that she had enough spirit to sing in the midst of all that horror." When Doug and Lisee asked me what would happen to Caterina, I told them if we didn't get her up to speed developmentally, there was a chance she could be sent to the home for "irrecuperables" where hundreds of children are just warehoused with very little attention. Within weeks they decided to try to adopt Caterina. When they started the process in June of 1991, the Romanian government closed down all adoptions for six months because of abuses in the private adoption system. Doug and Lisee had to do a "ton" of paperwork and every step along the way, they were told that they would never get her out. "The easiest way would be to quit, but we kept coming back to 'What about Caterina?'" Lisee reported. "I felt God must have wanted us to have her because otherwise why would we have found her?"

In May 1992, Dr. Barbara Bascomb went to the orphanage director, Dr. Birtz, and asked as a personal favor to let this one child be adopted. Dr. Birtz said she would give her permission to let Caterina go, but the birth mother had to be found, and she would have to agree for the adoption. This became a huge task for many reasons. First, there was limited information where the mother could be, the family had a history of moving to different cities. Second, the general fear of the culture, especially when someone is looking for you, was you must be in trouble. Doug and Lisee asked the help of some Romanian friends to try to find Caterina's mother. Weeks went by without any progress in finding the mother. Then one day, she showed up at the orphanage. I later found out that she was frightened because she heard the police were looking for her. I was leaving my building to go out to lunch with Monica when I saw a young woman standing in front of the entrance, looking somewhat lost. I immediately had a feeling that this could be the mother. When I asked if she was and she said yes. I told her to stay right there, and I excitedly ran off to get Monica to translate. The mother was young and quite pretty. She also appeared very anxious and didn't make any eye contact. Caterina's mother stated she didn't want to give Caterina up, but she had to because she had other children and could barely feed them. After a short conversation, the time came when it was time to ask the mother the all-important question. I remember thinking, just before I asked the question, that this answer will have an everlasting effect on this little girl's life. The mother answered yes, I sighed a breath of relief. The mother then said, "I hope Caterina will never mock me." Monica and I assured her that Caterina would never feel that way about her, and it took a lot of love to sign the papers. We told the mother that Doug and Lisee would make great parents for Caterina, and she would be well taken care of. It was a happy time but at the same time a sad time for us all.

After the adoption was finalized on December 11, 1992, Doug and Lisee flew to Romania, where they stayed with a local family. The new parents didn't want to rip Caterina from her environment, so they visited her every day. They used to take Caterina with her friend Stella to my office to play. That gained her trust. Next step was to take her outside her building in the park, which gradually went to a short visit outside the orphanage grounds. With a lot of love and understanding by Doug and Lisee, Caterina gained more confidence in her new surroundings and her new parents. The final step was a sleepover, where Doug and Lisee were staying. That experience went well. On January 3, Doug and Lisee came to the orphanage not to visit but to give her an opportunity of a lifetime, to leave the orphanage for good. Stella sensed that her good buddy was not coming back. Stella took Caterina's snowsuit and hid it behind a trunk. It was quite an emotional time for all of us, especially for poor Stella. Taking Caterina to the courtyard of the orphanage, we could see Stella's crying face pressed up against the window looking down at us. They took the train to Bucharest, where they had to stay four days to finalize all the paperwork. Then off to a beautiful home with her parents in Malibu. Doug and Lisee credit the advice of a child psychologist they went to when they got back to the United States with easing Caterina's adjustment. They made a book of snapshots of Caterina and Stella at the orphanage and photos of themselves and Caterina's new grandparents and the house. Lisee mentioned that Caterina would go through the picture book five times a day. I was told Caterina had problems sleeping, and they would stay with her until she fell asleep. But then she would wake up shrieking. "One day we heard her banging her head on the wall. Before we got up there, her head had gone through the drywall," Lisee said. The psychologist explained that children in that environment will get attention any way they can. They will go to extremes of behavior because negative attention is better than none.

With lots of love, patience, understanding, prayer, and professional help, Caterina did remarkably well. In a short time in her new home, she attended Malibu Presbyterian Day School. Lisee reported, "I thought I would have to be with Caterina at school the whole time. But she ran out into the playground and after forty-five minutes the teacher said, 'What are you hanging around for?'" Caterina really made a lot of progress in a very short period of time.

A few years later, World Vision moved its headquarters from California to Washington. Thus Doug, Lisee, and Caterina moved to Federal Way, Washington. I remember the day I looked after Caterina when Doug and Lisee were looking for a house. We had to go grocery shopping that day, so I took our small son Ted and Caterina to the store. Going down the aisles of the store with Caterina and Ted in the shopping cart was surreal. Just a few years ago, Caterina was just one of many kids on my floor in an orphanage in Romania, now we're shopping together with my son (I wasn't thinking about getting married when I arrived in Romania). I did God's will by going to Romania and gained so many blessings from it. I could have never imagined the shopping experience in a million years.

Here is a poem that Monica and I gave to Doug and Lisee.

> Dear Doug and Lisee,
> This poem really brings out how lucky Caterina is to have you.
>> Love,
>> Jeff and Monica

Offertory prayer from Sunday, October 9, in honor of the 25th Anniversary of the UCC Child Center:

> Blessed are the children
> Who bring us sticky kisses and fistfuls of dandelions,
> Who hug us in a hurry and forget their lunch money.
>
> And blessed are those
> Who never get dessert,
> Who have no safe blanket to drag behind them,
> Who can't find any bread to steal,
> Who don't have any rooms to clean up,
> Whose pictures aren't on anybody's dresser,
> whose monsters are real.
>
> Blessed are the children
> Who spend all their allowance before Tuesday,
> Who throw tantrums in the grocery store and pick
> at their food,
> Who like ghost stories,

Who shove dirty clothes under the bed and never
rinse out the tub,
Who get visits from the tooth fairy,
Who don't like to be kissed in front of the carpool,
Who squirm in church or temple and scream in
the phone
Whose tears we sometimes laugh at, whose smiles
can make us cry.

And blessed are those
Whose nightmares come in the daytime,
Who will eat anything,
Who have never seen a dentist,
Who aren't spoiled by anybody,
Who go to bed hungry and cry themselves to sleep,
Who live and move, but have no being.

Blessed are the children who want to be carried
And blessed are those who must,
Blessed are those we never give up on and those
Who don't get a second chance.

Blessed are those we smother . . . and those who
will grab
The hand of anybody kind enough to offer it.

Several years down the road, there was another experience involving Caterina that I could never have foreseen. I received a phone call from Caterina when she was in high school. She asked me if I could help her on a school project. She wanted to shadow me on my job as a children's crisis worker because she wanted to become a social worker. Caterina spent a day with me as I talked with kids and families in crisis. I believe that was a great experience for us both. Again, God's hand was in this. On May 15, 2011, Caterina received a bachelor of arts in sociology at Whitworth University in

Spokane, Washington. What an accomplishment for this wonderful young lady.

Caterina is currently working one-on-one with developmentally challenged students in the school system. Her supervisor has told Caterina that she really knows how to reach these kids. It appears that Caterina is sharing her blessings with others.

I learned many things from my Romanian experience. The most important was to follow where God leads you. You must spend time in prayer and reflection to know that it is God's will.

As I mentioned before, I made a pros and cons list about going to Romania. My logical brain said to stay home and my emotional/spiritual side told me to go. I wasn't 100 percent sure that this was what God wanted me to do when I made the decision to go to Romania. In the few weeks that followed my decision, the doors opened when I found out World Vision was sending professionals out in Romania in the next two months. After an interview and a check of my records, I was going to Romania. It sure looked like God's will now. I was single, didn't have any financial obligations, so I was free to go. God picked the right moment for me. I'm so glad that I listened.

I learned so much from the warm and kind Romanian people. Most of them didn't have too much but were very generous in all the wonderful meals and friendship they gave me. Thursday dinners at Mama George's with her son Cristi was always a highlight of the week. Cristi's friendship through the two years in Cluj was quite a blessing and learning experience. He helped me to understand the Romanian culture. I also learned not to take things so seriously from Cristi and to keep laughing, even at myself and my American ways. He introduced me to his friends; in a short time, I had a group of guy friends. I learned the true meaning of being a good neighbor. Turi and Veturia with their families looked after me in the apartment complex we lived in. At times when I was sick, they gave me Romanian remedies that worked like a charm. On Sundays I would come over in the evening to Turi's apartment to watch an American movie on TV. The warmth of their families really made me feel accepted and loved.

I learned so much from the children of the orphanage. They showed me resiliency and a determination to keep growing despite the odds against them. I learned how precious children are to us all. We need to nurture them with kindness and understanding. Just watching them develop gave me a great sense of joy. To see them change the lives of staff was truly amazing.

I gained so much from my experience in Romania that definitely affected my life in so many ways. I'm so glad that I listened to God's call.

I have been back to Romania in 2004 and 2015 with Monica and Ted. Monica has been back five other times. On visiting the orphanage in 2004, there were about half as many children as in 1993 when I left. There were still some Romanian caregivers in the orphanage being paid by World Vision. I met with a local organization that was helping place children into foster care. We also met Stella, Caterina's friend, who was now sixteen years old and still living in the orphanage. She had her own room and was learning a profession at a trade school in the city.

In 2015, there were no children living permanently at the orphanage. A small group of children lived there on a short-term emergency basis before they were placed with a family. The director told us that there was now a law stating that no child from birth to three years old would be sent to an orphanage to live on a long-term basis. They would be set up with a foster family. Many of the rooms that previously housed the children were now remodeled into offices that had various programs for children.

The orphanage in 2015 again was silent. You didn't hear any children's voices, but unlike in 1991 when I first arrived, this was a good thing. Most children are now set up with families that will love them and give them a chance in life.

St. Michael's Church, where we got married (middle and right picture)

Playroom when I first arrived

Playroom six months later

Top floor of orphanage before remodel

Top floor of Orphanage after the La Canada's remodel

The artists from England surprised me by painting my office door.

Hello Marcel

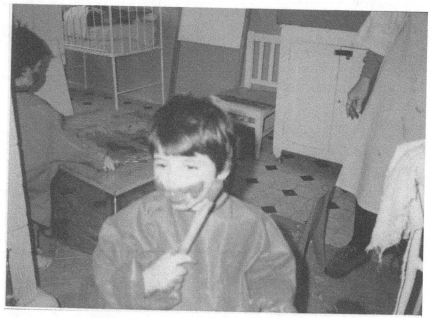

Painting activity turned into face painting

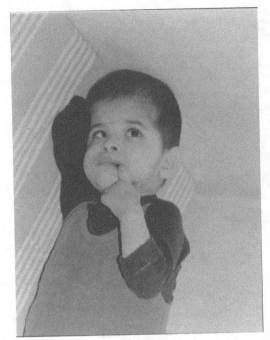

Woarda

Giovana's third birthday with Teacher Jenny

Fun in the sun with the new playground equipment

Potty time, have anything to read?

Okay guys, let's get organized!

Making the magazine cover with Roxanna

Doug, Lisee, Caterina leaving the orphanage
for the last time, January 1993

Caterina and Teddy in the same grocery cart in Edmonds,
Washington, only God could of made this happen.

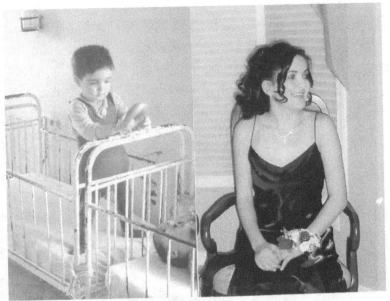

Caterina at two years old. Caterina at high school prom

Getting married with Monica, December 7, 1991 at St. Michael's Church
Best-man Cristi, Maid-of-honor Olimpia, best-man Nelu, maid-
of-honor Carman and two wonderful priests (Left to Right)

Family Group
Olimpia, Maria, Stefi, Me, Monica, Stefan, Marcela,
Oli, Monica's Dad and Mom (Left to Right)

Pig celebration, care for some ear?

3

SCHOOL

"It is not good to have zeal without knowledge,
nor to be hasty and miss the way"
(Prov. 19:2).

I attended Sacred Heart Villa, a Catholic school run by nuns who were short in stature but packed a wallop. Dressed in all black, it was their way or a tug on your earlobe. I was full of energy and back then was considered a disruptive child. One teacher reported to my parents that I even danced to the pencil sharpener. I went to Assumption School through grades six and seven because the nuns had had it with me at Sacred Heart. Assumption was another Catholic school, but it had laypeople as teachers. I did better there, with average grades, but I remained high-spirited and I still found it hard to focus in the classroom. I remember many times coming in from recess with a ripped shirt, full of sweat from the various games we played.

Next stop was a public middle school, Nathan Eckstein, for eighth and ninth grades. That's where I met my best friend, Newy. The first day of school, we couldn't open our lockers so we had to go to the office for help. And so the two knuckleheads became friends.

Still not experiencing a lot of academic success, but I wasn't dancing to the pencil sharpener any longer. I made some good friends at Nathan Eckstein and enjoyed the teachers. Track became my identity at school. I remember during one of the first days of school, I was standing in line at the cafeteria when two black boys approached me. The tallest boy, who I later learned was Gerald Singletary, claimed to be the fastest boy in the school. He challenged me to a race right then and there. I got the feeling that he wouldn't take no for an answer. So off we went behind the school and raced about fifty yards, which he won. I guess word of my track accomplishments had preceded me to Nathan Eckstein. In seventh grade, I won the 75-yard dash in the Catholic Youth Organization (CYO) championships. Later in the week the track coach was asking me to turn out. For the next two years, Gerald Singletary was still the fastest, with me being the second fastest at the school. I used to hand off to him on the relay teams. We hardly ever lost in two years. Though still not the smartest in school, I was definitely one of the fastest. Slow in one area, but fast in another.

It was expected that I would go to a public high school after ninth grade. Having average grades with some classes below average, that was my destiny. A good friend who was also a runner went to Bishop Blanchet, a Catholic high school. Tim "Sully" Sullivan talked to the track coach about my times, and suddenly I was also going to Blanchet. It shocked my mom and dad when I told them I was going to Blanchet. They must have been wondering, "How did you pull that off?" I spent a good three years there; track again served as my identity. Our track coach was Mr. Ed Thenell, who died too young at the age of thirty-six. He was looking into some possible track scholarships for me at the end of my senior year, but with a GPA of 1.9 from high school, there weren't any offers. If they had presented a Least Likely to Become a Doctor Award in my senior year, I would have been a leading contender.

My next academic stop was Shoreline Community College. I took business classes there for two years but really wasn't that excited about the subject matter. What I was excited about was going out with the boys on the weekends. Let the beer and the good times flow! The summer after my second year at Shoreline, I spent two months in Europe backpacking through several countries with Newy.

In Europe, I was impressed with all the fine hotels, even though we didn't stay in any of them. At home in Washington, I had worked in a hotel where my dad was a managing owner. I returned home from Europe and told my folks I wanted to go to a university that had a major in hotel administration. My dad helped me out, but with only six weeks before school started, how could I get in? We first tried Cornell University, which was an Ivy League school. Looking back at that now, I don't know what I was thinking. That hope didn't last long.

We found out that there was a hotel school in Las Vegas that was still accepting students. So with two weeks before school started, I flew down with my dad and my low two-point-something GPA from community college to visit the University of Nevada at Las Vegas (UNLV). Somehow my dad arranged a meeting with the Dean of Hotel Administration and by Dad's fast talking and the grace of God, I got in. Now the only thing I needed to do was find a place to stay. The dorms would be perfect, right on campus, with a built-in social network. Reality set in: Because I had registered so late, the dorms were full. I was disappointed, because I didn't want to be the lonely guy in a single apartment.

Then it came to me, why not see the track coach? My running had gotten me into Blanchet, why not the dorms too? My dad dropped me off at the track office and waited outside. An hour later, I came out and Dad had a big smile on his face. He later told me that he thought I had a long talk with the track coach and my housing problems were now over. What really happened was that there was a line to see Assistant Coach Al McDaniels, and I got only a few minutes with him. All the dorm rooms were full for his scholarship runners. Coach Al said I could come on out as a walk-on, and he could get me a pair of shoes. I would have preferred to have a place to stay and buy my own shoes! Such is life. *Well, that didn't work out the way I planned.*

My dad tried to cheer me, but I was down in the dumps and anxious about my rooming situation. So off we went to the school cafeteria to have lunch. While perusing the school newspaper, my dad read an article about fraternities that were rushing potential brothers. I remember the first thing I thought was *Not me. I don't want to be with a bunch of rah-rah guys singing silly songs and dressing alike.* My dad gave me the look that said, "What other options do you have?" After I calmed down and thought about it, I knew that he was right.

I picked the first frat on the list, Sigma Chi, and called. I was told to come on over. The frat house was a two-story small building on the edge of the desert. The guys seemed nice, but most importantly there was an empty bed. So I was in and ready to pledge. My plan was to stay the semester, then get into the dorm or move into an apartment with some guys I would meet in school. Sigma Chi became a good fit for me and was not the fraternity stereotype I had envisioned of a bunch of brainless guys who sat around and drank beer all day. I stayed at Sigma Chi my whole three years, because most of my brothers were well-rounded guys.

The brothers still liked to have parties at the house on the weekends. I was the social chairman for my first year. I guess I put on good parties, because the next year I was voted President (Counsel) of the fraternity. Going away to school made me more outgoing and allowed me to try different things. Getting out of my comfort zone was the best thing for me.

I tried to get into student government during my junior year at UNLV. I ran for Senator representing the Hotel School. Three of us ran and the first two were picked. I came in third or dead last, you could say. I used the nickname the fraternity gave me: Bugs. I campaigned hard, spoke at rallies, put up signs, and spread the word. At the end, I didn't make it. *Maybe next time I'll go by my real name,* I thought. The next year I did run again, this time for Treasurer of the School. My new slogan for the race was "Bank on Baird." With the backing of the fraternity and the Student Government President Joe Gariffa, I won. Being the treasurer of the school had its benefits: I had my own office in the Student Union, a shared secretary, and my tuition paid. I could give back my track scholarship to help my team. If I had gone to school around home, I know I wouldn't be in student government or in a fraternity. I would be hanging out with my same friends, doing the same things. At UNLV, I made four types of friends: one group from the track team, another from student government, another from the frat, and one from my classes.

I went to UNLV for three years. In total, it took me five years to graduate with a bachelor of science (BS) degree in hotel administration. My grades at UNLV were not stellar. I had mostly Cs, with a few Ds and Bs. I did get one A, in psychology; maybe that was a sign for things to come.

My parents and sister flew in to Las Vegas for the graduation. Frank Sinatra received an honorary doctorate and was the commencement speaker. Only in Las Vegas! I had a "Jeff is finally getting out of school" party at Caesar's Palace. A fellow Sigma Chi was in upper management there and saw that I got a beautiful suite, the one you see in the movies with the piano. It was a great party. Even Coach Al and the president of the University were there. A great mix of people, and everyone just fit in and had a good time. When my family was coming to town, I asked a friend named Buddy to put up "Welcome Cool Bairds" on the outside reader board in front of the university. Thinking back, I could have gotten in a lot of trouble for that. When we drove by the sign, my parents and sister were shocked. "How did you do that?" Buddy was a student who worked at the Student Union as a janitor. Through the years we became friends, so naturally he was invited to my getting-out-of-college party. He met my parents and other friends. When it was time to take my family back to the airport, we went by UNLV for the last time and to see the "Welcome Cool Bairds" sign one more time. It was taken down when we arrived, only to be replaced by "Goodbye Cool Bairds." Buddy had done this, all on his own!

My next academic stop was the University of Hawaii at Manoa, where I was taking one psychology class per quarter just to see if my curiosity was still there. No pressure, just learning because of my interest. I was working fifty hours a week at the Ilikai Hotel as a manager of Annabelle's. I took classes during the day and worked till early in the morning.

Through prayer, I needed to map out my next direction. With God's guidance, and the support of my parents, I decided to go full time at the University to take all the classes needed to apply to graduate school in psychology. I left a good-paying job at Annabelle's because I thought I was following God's will in changing courses. By the next week, I was taking classes full-time and working at the state mental hospital as a nursing aide. I needed to make some money to pay for my expenses, even though my parents were helping me out.

I did my year at University of Hawaii taking undergraduate psychology classes. To help raise my grades, I completed every extra credit assignment available. In the psychology department they were always looking for human subjects to test for research experiments. I was the number-one guinea pig for the doctoral students. I really enjoyed my classes, especially abnormal psychology. The human brain was fascinating to study.

One class, though, was very difficult for me and I had to take it two times: statistics. With the help of a tutor and studying very hard, I got through the statistics class the second time. I even set it up so that my stats professor was a guest judge at one of the contests at Annabelle's. I would have loved to stay in Hawaii for grad school, but I knew my chances were slim to get into the clinical psychology program at the University of Hawaii. They only took a handful of students each year. I looked for a school where I had better odds.

I searched for several weeks until I found the California School of Professional Psychology (CSPP), a nonprofit educational institution. Established in 1970, CSPP had a philosophy to create a unique community for professional training that was kept small and stimulating. They had four California campuses: Berkeley, Fresno, Los Angeles, and San Diego. Still not easy to get into, I thought that CSPP was my best chance to get a PhD in clinical psychology and become a psychologist, although at the time I didn't know how to spell psychologist!

CSPP wanted you to pick your top schools in order. I picked Fresno as my top pick, not because I really wanted to go to school in that city, but I felt it wouldn't be a top pick of a lot of students, so I would increase my chances. I flew in from Hawaii for the interview and by the grace of God, I got in! Miracles can happen! Through CSPP, I found a roommate with whom I could share an apartment. I also learned that he was good at math. *This could be the beginning of a beautiful relationship!* When I drove to Fresno for the start of the school year, I was thinking it was so great that I had a place to stay and a roommate, unlike when I started at UNLV. However, when I arrived at the apartment and knocked, I noticed through the window a pair of women's shoes. Not a good sign. As I soon found out, his girlfriend was living at the apartment. She had told him the relationship was off unless she went along to Fresno with him. He told me he was sorry, but what could he do?

I spent that night in a motel. In three days, my graduate school adventure was about to begin and I didn't even have a permanent place to stay. Through prayer, I calmed myself down somewhat. I still couldn't completely let all the stress go. (Even now, I am still working on surrendering 100 percent to the Lord.) Soon, I found an apartment with orange carpet and yellow and orange furniture. I felt that I was living inside a pumpkin. Home Sweet Home!

September of 1985: I was thirty-two years old and ready to begin another journey in the world of academics. This time, I would be with students who have already written professional articles in psychology and worked in the mental health field in various settings. I was nervous about how I would do with all these big hitters. Leaning on faith in a loving God, support financially and emotionally from my mom and dad ("You can do it, Jeffo!"), and encouragement from my sister and her family and my friends, I was ready to do my best and see what happens.

CSPP/Fresno had a few hundred students. The classes I would have to take were in the areas of physiological psychology, advanced statistics, learning, developmental psychology, social psychology, personality, intellectual and personality assessment, projective techniques, community psychology, abnormal psychology, psychotherapy, psychopharmacology, clinical sexology, and child abuse and reporting.

Everyone was friendly, and I soon met Alan and Franko, who would become very good friends. Through the school year, we tried to drink some beer and play pool once a week. I remember my first presentation for a class; it was on panic attacks. I was anxious before the talk because this was graduate school, so it had to be at an upper level. There were thirty students listening to my speech. At the end,

I faked having a panic attack to demonstrate how one looked. I liked doing presentations with a flair, like the time in high school when we had to give a speech on how to do something. With the permission of the teacher (a good sport), I demonstrated how to take your clothes off before bed. I took off my shirt, and when it came to my pants, the students were wide-eyed, probably thinking "He won't take off his pants." Well, I did, but I had gym shorts on underneath. Or the time I was working at Annabelle's and was asked to give a speech to the business students about the disco industry. The presentation was on how to be an effective manager. When the professor said my name, I came in from the hall, with disco music playing and two dancing women on each arm. We danced around for a moment, then I began my talk on the life of a disco manager. The heart of the talk was that there was much more to running a successful night spot than just dancing around being cool; it's about making money and managing your resources.

Back to CSPP, I really enjoyed most of the classes and, surprise, I did fairly well. But my old nemesis came back to haunt me: statistics. I had to take a full year of stats. I struggled through and passed both classes through prayer and lots of hard work. Looking back, I got through the course but I still really didn't understand it.

During my first year at CSPP, I heard an interesting rumor about one of our professors. His name was Dr. Wes Forbes and he would later become a member of my dissertation committee. The story goes that Dr. Forbes used to be a member of a doo-wop singing group called the Five Satins. They were known for their hit song "In the Still of the Night," which sold over two million records in the late 1950s. I had heard of the song and being a blues and soul fan, I had to find out if it was true. One day after class, I saw Dr. Forbes walking to his car, and I ran up to him. I began singing "In the still of the night . . ." I asked him did he record that song with the Five Satins? He smiled and said he did, but it didn't sound like that!

At the middle of the second year, the school had a comprehensive exam in four areas: clinical psychology, social and learning maturation, personality, and statistics. You had three chances in each area. If you failed one area three times, you would be expelled from school. Students would receive their master's degree but couldn't go ahead for the PhD. Test-taking has never been my strong point, and with stats looming over me again, I was anxious about how well I would do. I pledged to myself that the only way that I wouldn't get my PhD was to get kicked out of school.

The first time around, I passed one area and failed three areas. My study buddies, my golf-playing, pool-shooting friends, did a lot better than I did. Each new exam I took was different from the last one. So I kept chipping away at it, passing another, failing one. Eventually it got down to it: stats and me again. I failed the first two stats comps with ease. Even with joining a stats study group and doing my own review, I didn't pass. After studying for a few months, I took it again. The stats group was no longer available when I went for my third time because they had all passed. The instructor of the study group, Dr. Gordon Cappelletty, was now seeing me on an individual basis. God bless him, he had so much patience with me. He never lost his temper, though it seemed at times he was about to blow his lid.

The night before my third try, I felt calm because I had put it into God's hands. I asked for his blessing and asked him to guide me through whatever outcome came about. The next day, I gave it my best and thought I had a good chance of passing. I had to wait a week for the results. Did I finally get over the stats hump? No, I failed for the third time. I was extremely disappointed. I received a letter shortly after from CSPP.

> Dear Jeff,
> The Faculty met on Friday, June 12, 1987, to review the academic standing of all students.
>
> Based on your failure of the Area II Preliminary Examinations for the third time, the Faculty recommended your termination from the program.
> The Faculty would like you to know this decision was not made lightly or without con-

siderable deliberation. The Faculty recommendation is final, however, if you choose to appeal the
decision, you may do so. The appeal is directed
to Dr. Gary Cannon, Provost.

If we can be of any assistance in the appeal
process, please feel free to contact either me or
Linda Witt.

Sincerely,
Mary Beth Kenkel, PhD
Dean for Academic & Professional Affairs

I could appeal the expulsion! Back on my knees again: *"Okay,
Lord, what's next?"* Through God's guidance and the fighting Baird
spirit, I appealed the decision. I got letters of recommendation from
past internship supervisors and the manager at my current job, working with brain-injured adults. I sent in the letters, with a personal
letter asking for one more try. My clinical work was excellent and
I felt I could make a good psychologist. I turned everything in and
waited for a reply.

Several days later, I was told to be at the president's office the
next day. When I arrived, he stated that after reading the letters of
recommendation and my own letter, he would grant me one more
try at the comps. But, he stated, if I failed for the fourth time, there
would be no appeals, and I would be out. He handed me a letter
stating what he had just said.

Dear Jeff:

After reviewing your case and the letters of
support which were sent to me on your behalf,
I have decided to support your petition to be
allowed one final opportunity to take the Statistic
Preliminary Exam.

The responsible and professional way in
which you presented your case and the very
supportive letters which I received from Drs.
O'Connor and Cappelletty in addition to your

excellent course work and field placement performance, all combined to present a strong argument in favor of this exception.

In addition to continuing your tutoring
with Dr. Cappelletty, I would encourage you to
work on the death anxiety issue in your personal
psychotherapy. Should you be unable to pass the
exam on the next trial, as you know, you would
immediately be terminated from the program.

I wish you the best of luck during this next
academic year.

Sincerely,
W. Gary Cannon, PhD
Provost

I was thankful, but in a daze driving home. When I looked at the
letter more closely, there was a part saying I had "death anxiety." When
I called his office to clarify, I was told it should have read "test anxiety,"
so they changed that part of the letter. I surely wasn't going to die over
stats, but yes, with my past performances, I was definitely nervous!

The day of reckoning came: the comprehensive statistics exam.
I felt I was as ready as I could be. With lots more studying, tutoring
with Gordon, great support from family and friends, and prayer, let's
get it on! When I got the exam, as always, I briefly looked it over. I
do this to try to pace myself and not run out of time. After a quick
scan, I knew I was going to pass, maybe because this was my fourth
time and they could only change the questions so much. With the
grace of God, I did pass.

MEMORANDUM
TO: Jeff Baird
FROM: Linda G. Witt, Registrar
RE: Preliminary Examinations
As you may know, you:
____X____ DID PASS Area(s) II Data Analysis/
Research Design

You can only imagine how happy I was! I invited my friends and Gordon to a local bar to celebrate. I had planned a surprise in advance that night. When everyone arrived and we had just finished our first round of drinks, a man dressed in black with a cap on went to Gordon and said, "Dr. Cappelletty, your limo is ready." At first he thought the driver got the wrong guy, but when he looked over and saw me smiling, then he knew for sure that I was behind it. Off we went for a night of partying. The cost of the limo and drinks set me back some, thus I had chili and beans for a while, but it was worth it.

From then on, getting my PhD at CSPP was downhill because I could control the outcome with hard work and doing extra credit assignments. For most classes, you had to write some papers, do a presentation, and take some quizzes. I liked all the clinical subject matter a lot, so it didn't seem so much like a chore, just a steady grind.

Speaking of a slow process that at times feels like it will never end, that describes the writing of the doctoral dissertation. Coming up with the topic was fairly easy for me. I made the switch from hotel and restaurant management to psychology because I wanted to work with kids and families as a psychologist. So what would be the worst thing that could happen to a young person? If the person kills themselves, there is no hope left to turn around a life. The title of my dissertation was "The Relationship between Suicide Risk, Hopelessness, Depression, and Religious Commitment." The dedication read, "This dissertation is dedicated with love to my Mom and Dad, the wind beneath my wings." My favorite part of the dissertation was the writing of the Acknowledgments, when I wrote:

Acknowledgments

Writing this part of the dissertation is a joy; there are no statistics, revisions, collecting and scoring of data, or citing numerous researchers involved, just a chance to express my deepest appreciation to the many who have given so much. This research has not been a one-year project with thanks now coming at the end, but this is the result of five years of training, guidance, and support from some of the very best researchers, clinicians, and friends I have ever known. To give the proper credit due to everyone, I would need to write an entire dissertation (and I refuse to do that again), so I hope you will all know how much I truly appreciate your help and support.

First and foremost, I would like to give thanks to God, whose guidance and support helped me through the winding roads of graduate school and made my hypotheses concerning religion come out as being significant (it is a good idea to have Him in your corner). I would like to express appreciation to my committee chairperson, Fred Cutter, a giant among giants in the field of suicidology. His knowledge, support, and faith in me were extremely important in enabling me to complete this project. I wish to thank my two other committee members: Rosemary Papalewis, who got down in the trenches with me and methodically went over every word of my dissertation—her enthusiasm, patience, knowledge of research, and gentle warmth were invaluable; Wes Forbes, who helped me cut down my original, grandiose amount of variables to a more manageable number—his influence on obtaining subjects, humor, and deep interest were a great comfort. Special thanks to my statistical wizard, Gordon Cappelletty, for his never ending patience and time.

I have been extremely fortunate to have the encouragement, support, and assistance of many friends and colleagues. I would especially like to thank Rose Chapa for her endless support and caring, who hung in there with me when my mind was in the research clouds. Thanks to Alan "Dr. Z" Zimmerman and Franko Abreau, my fellow classmates, who always kept me laughing and headed in the right direction. Thanks to Linda Witt, whose guidance and support helped me get through the comprehensives and thus the opportunity of even writing a dissertation. Thanks to Kita Curry, a great role model on how a clinical psychologist should be, who gave me the support and guidance at my internship, which enabled me the peace of mind to finish this research. Special thanks to Mary Jane Cavanaugh, who did more than just type this manuscript; she turned a pile of scattered papers into a masterpiece. Her knowledge and advice to always keep your suit jacket on during the final orals, no matter how hot it is, will always be remembered.

A special citation and thanks to all the wonderful administrators who granted me approval to go into their high schools and believed in this project. Thanks to the teachers whose cooperation and support made the testing process go smoothly. Thanks to all the parents who gave permission for their teenagers to partake in this study. A special thanks to the students who gave up their time to take yet another test.

There is a handful of special people to whom I am deeply indebted for their emotional support throughout this and many other academic adventures: To my best friend, Ted "Newy" Newman, who was always on my side even when I was wrong; to Janner Flom, my Hawaii study buddy, who believed in me long before I did; to my sister, Mary Ann, who stood by me in the darkest hours.

The results of my research study were as follows: The negative correlation between religious commitment and suicide risk indicated that as religious commitment is higher, suicide risk tends to be lower. The negative correlation between religious commitment and hopelessness indicated that as religious commitment is higher, hopelessness tends to be lower. Describing the results further, I wrote:

> The Christian school students scored the lowest on depression and hopelessness and second lowest on suicide risk. Students from the public continuation school scored higher on suicide risk and hopelessness than students from the public high SES [socioeconomic status], public middle SES, and private Christian high schools. The public continuation students scored the lowest on religious commitment. One could infer from these results that religion could be an important variable in the maintenance of a healthy mental status.
>
> The contribution of grades in school gave significant results. Students who usually received low grades were at higher risk for suicide risk, depression, and hopelessness than were the students who received higher grades. Students who received As and Bs tended to be most religious, while students with poor grades tended to be less religious.
>
> Suicide risk and depression had a significant relationship with ethnic group. The non-Caucasian students were significantly higher on suicide risk and depression than the Caucasian students. Ethnicity had no apparent effect on either hopelessness or religious commitment.

The dissertation, school work, and passing the comprehensive exams were all part of the process of getting my PhD. In addition, I completed various internships throughout the five years it took me to get my degree. My first internship was at an elementary school, where I learned to administer IQ tests. Between testing, I just hung out with the kids and played. No serious clinical work was done; indeed, at this point I wouldn't have known what that entailed anyway.

The second semester of the first year, January of 1986, I began my next field placement, which was at Wakefield Juvenile Hall. My supervisor was Dave Halpern. He was very knowledgeable about how to work with juvenile offenders. Mr. Halpern had a laid-back approach, which had a calming effect on all who worked with him. I really enjoyed the experience of working with a population that society has deemed unacceptable. When I went to my site each day, I truly enjoyed being locked up. I was excited to be in a challenging and potentially dangerous environment. The teens I saw had been charged with a wide array of crimes; most were in gangs. I did psychological testing with them. Hopefully some of the information gained will help the professionals working with them in the future.

In my second year at CSPP, we had to do a twenty-hour-a-week internship for both semesters. I chose Konkel School, which was in the Fresno Unified School District. The school served adolescents between the ages of twelve and eighteen who were experiencing emotional distress serious enough to significantly impair their ability to form healthy relationships with others. My supervisor was Tim Sabo, the psychologist at the school. He gave me a lot of freedom to figure out what I was doing, but he also was knowledgeable and supportive. My role was to do therapy with several of the kids on a weekly basis. Although I had now taken some classes on doing therapy and I received supervision on my therapy work, actually doing therapy was still a new concept for me. So I took walks around the school with each of my students and listened to what they had to say. All of them came from chaotic and abusive families; drug abuse and alcoholism among family members was very common. Each teen had a story to tell and I learned to listen and not judge. The students taught me many things, an important one being resilience.

Konkel School had a student paper and I responded to students' letters in a Dear Abby format as "Miss Understanding." My identity was not disclosed to the students.

Dear Miss Understanding:

I have a problem with a girl and she will talk to me but she does not know I like her and I do want her to know but I do not want her to think I am a jerk or pushy. How can I let her know my feelings.

Sincerely,
Screwed Up

Dear Screwed Up:

Action speaks louder than words. If you are nice to her, smile when she goes by and have some kind words for her. I believe she will get the picture. Being concerned about being too forward is a smart concern because it turns off a lot of girls. Asking her if you two could work on a school assignment could be an easy way to spend more time with her. Also try to find out what she likes to do and suggest doing one of those activities with her.

It takes more than saying "I like you" to another person for them to feel the same way about you. Showing the person you care and are very interested in their welfare will speak louder than words.

Dear Miss Understanding:

I have a problem with some of my old friends that are a bad influence on me, but they keep bugging me to hang around with them, but if I do I know I'll get in trouble one way or another. But I cannot seem to tell them to leave me alone. What should I do.

Confused

Dear Confused:

How to deal with friends that are bad influences? You bring up a very good question that many students are faced with. Everyone wants to be a part of the crowd and to have friends. We all want to be liked and accepted. The problem arises when friends want you to test your loyalty by doing things that get you into trouble, like taking drugs, running away from home or skipping school. One thing you might do is try not to hang around places where you might get into trouble. Explore new activities and interests where you can meet new friends. Also a part time job could help you earn extra money but also could be a good place to meet new friends and keep you busy after school.

A past president of the United States said: "The buck stops here." You might be pressured by your old friends to get into trouble but you are the one that has to make the final decision. If you have to do certain things like taking drugs, to be someone's friend, he or she really isn't a friend. Stand firm on what you believe is right, you'll be a stronger person for it.

Dear Miss Understanding:

Recently at my residential home a mistake happened and it wasn't my fault at all. This is what happened. I came home from school one day and the staff thought I was acting strange, they thought that I might be on drugs. They gave me a UA (urine test for drugs). The test came back positive with PCP in it. I never did PCP in my life and hadn't done any drugs recently. As a result, for having PCP in my urine they didn't give me my status and didn't give me my furlo (home visit) and their trust level in me has gone way down. What should I do about this?

Mixed up & mistaken

Dear Mixed Up & Mistaken:

The issue here is not who is right or wrong, only you know that for sure. The many events in our life don't always turn out the way we would like it. I imagine that you have already voiced your side of the story to the staff at the residential home. Try to understand now that what is done, is done and mistaken or not you have to live with the results. I would suggest to hang in there and in a short period of time, your status and trust should start to build in the staff eyes if you stay out of trouble. Try not to let this set back give you the "Oh, what is the use" type of attitude. Because if you start to get into a lot of trouble, you are just telling the staff that they were right all along.

My next internship was at Fresno City College. My supervisor was Bob Richardson, who was the psychologist at Fresno City College. I learned some interventions from Dr. Richardson that I still use today. This was the first time that I met people in an office environment as practicing therapists do. Two other interns and I even shared a receptionist, who greeted our clients. The whole thing was pretty exciting but at the same time a little scary. I was thinking *I hope I have something helpful to say*. It went better than I thought. I just listened, showed them I understood their problems, and offered a little advice if needed. I was energized after a day at Fresno City. I saw more clients than I was contracted for because I got such great satisfaction from being with someone in their time of need.

In therapy, I was beginning to use some of the theories I was learning in school, like cognitive behavioral therapy (CBT). I knew a little about several different theories. Most importantly, I was finding out that if you had a genuine concern about the person, they picked that up from you, and this helped bring about change.

After spending three years at the CSPP campus doing course work, going through the stages of my dissertation, and doing part-time internships, it was time to do a full-time internship. My fourth year would entail working full time at an internship that I applied for and was lucky enough to be offered. It even paid $12,000 a year! That was big bucks compared to what I was making at my previous internships: zero. I would be spending a year at Hathaway Children Village, which provided residential treatment and special education to severely emotionally disturbed children. Located in the foothills above the San Fernando Valley, the children's village stands on the former site of Cecil B. DeMille's Paradise Ranch. Children between five and eighteen years of age reside in the children's village.

With class work done and the difficult comprehensive exams behind me, I could now just concentrate on doing my internship and finishing my dissertation. I needed to move closer to the San Fernando Valley. I was fortunate to find an apartment in Glendale that a Hathaway intern had previously used for the year. I could buy the furniture in the apartment at a low price from her and basically just move in.

I soon found that Hathaway was exactly where I wanted to be. It was exciting to begin my work there, and at the same time I was wondering, *What in the world have I gotten myself into?* I would be under the supervision of Kita Curry, psychologist at Hathaway. Dr. Curry turned out to be a very skilled clinician and just as important, a patient and supportive person. My two fellow interns were Marian Williams and Roland Thompkins. They became great friends to me but they were both married, so there wasn't too much social time together.

I had a caseload of six teenage girls. Four were African-American, one Hispanic, and one Caucasian. Five out of the six girls grew up in some rough neighborhoods in LA. So here I go, a thirty-five-year-old white male who was going to do "therapy" on some street-smart girls. I wasn't of the mindset that I could save these girls. Rather, I was hoping that by working with them, I could gain their trust and help them in some small way.

How did it start out? Painfully! After a few days of the honeymoon period where the girls were just feeling me out, I thought, *This won't be so difficult.* Then, boom! I got it! The girls had received more therapy themselves than I had given to others. This was going to be a learning experience, with me doing most of the learning. One of my girls in therapy was a twin and her sister was also at Hathaway. I remember during the first week, she came up to me and said if I didn't treat her sister right, she would kick my ass. Most of the girls had a lot of pain and anger pent up, and guess who got it when things didn't go their way? The staff.

For the first few months, I personalized my girls' anger. They said many hurtful and mean things to me and I let them stick. During the first few weeks at Hathaway, while driving home, I felt I was the worst therapist in the world. As the months went by, I began to see how traumatic their lives had been. Most had never had a male figure in their life who had treated them well. I began making progress when I thought less about how I was doing as a therapist and became more concerned with really hearing their stories. It settled down throughout the year, with an occasional explosion of anger.

With the internship winding down, Dr. Curry told me we would be having a goodbye party for the interns. I told Dr. Curry we really didn't need a party, no need to spend the time and effort on it. She turned to me with a wise look on her face and said, "The party really is not for you, it's for the girls."

After I finished my internship year at Hathaway, I really had a place in my heart for the girls I had seen almost daily. During my last session with one of the girls, who had really given me a hard time, I noticed that she had tears in her eyes. When I asked her what she was feeling, she replied that she would miss me because now she would have to break in another therapist. It just makes you feel warm and fuzzy, doesn't it? I know I learned more from my girls than I offered them. God bless them all.

I moved back to Seattle for a few months, then I was off to Romania for two years. After my Romania years, I returned to the

States married and looking for an institution where I could complete my post-doctorate hours, which are required for psychologist licensure in the state of Washington. I was blessed to have a supervisor whom I had had in the past. Dr. Lisa Kahn, psychologist, was now working at the University of Washington in the mental retardation and rehabilitation clinics. She became my supervisor again, and I strictly did testing of children, mostly from two years old to ten years of age. Families from all over Washington state and nearby states came to have their children tested by an interdisciplinary team, which included doctors and interns from the fields of psychology, pediatrics, occupational therapy, and speech therapy. The UW clinic was a very stimulating work environment, with some great minds, and at times it could be somewhat intimidating for this ex-disco manager.

Besides getting my post-doc hours done, which would take me a year, I found another job at Compass Health as a Children's Crisis Worker to try to make ends meet. At this same time, I began studying for the state comprehensive exams. To call yourself a psychologist, you must pass a national written exam of two hundred multiple-choice questions. The passing rate was set at 70 percent, which seemed doable, but approximately one-third of applicants fail the first time taking it. The exam covered a wide array of psychological areas, including my favorite subject area, statistics! The test was given every six months in Olympia, Washington. If you passed the written exam, you could schedule an oral exam, which if you passed, you could then call yourself a psychologist.

With doing my post-doc hours at UW, working full-time at Compass as a Children's Outreach Worker, and beginning a family—our son was born February 7, 1994—I began preparing myself for the psychology written exam. I purchased a licensure preparation course, which entailed several workbooks and various practice tests. I didn't know it at the time, but it would take me four years to pass the written exam. It wasn't for lack of trying. I spent hundreds of hours at the local library. You could take the exam as many times as you want, but as I mentioned, you would have to wait another six months to take it again after failing. Each time that I received the "We regret to inform you that you failed" letter, for a total of seven separate times, it was difficult for a few days. Yet never once did I have the thought, *I'll just quit.* With my faith, my supportive wife, family, and friends, I was back with a new study plan very soon after receiving each letter of doom.

My sister, Mary Ann, wrote me a meaningful, supportive letter during this time.

> Dear Jeffo:
>
> Yes, I have finally figured out how to use our computer which has been a blessing because my handwriting is so hard to read. Anyway, I am not writing to demonstrate my word processing skills. I am writing because I spoke with Mom today and she gave me the news.
>
> Jeffo, words can't begin to describe how sorry I was . . . so I won't try except to say I will keep praying. Also, I want to include some words I recently read that remind me of you. I am reading a book about golf pros (Scott is so happy). In the book, Tom Watson uses an excerpt from Theodore Roosevelt's famous "Man in the Arena" speech to inspire his Ryder Cup team. Tom Watson loved this excerpt so much he had it taped to his bathroom mirror. Jeff, you may know it already, but I really thought of you when I read the words so I am going to repeat them now.
>
> It is not the critic who counts, not the one who points out how the strong man stumbled or how the doer of deeds might have done them better. The credit belongs to the man who is actually in the arena; whose face is marred with sweat and dust and blood; who strives valiantly; who errs and comes short again and again; who knows the great enthusiasms, the great devotions and spends himself in a worthy cause and

who, if he fails, at least fails while bearing greatly so that his place shall never be with those cold and timid souls who know neither victory nor defeat.

To me, Jeff, you have always been the man in the arena—fighting the fight. Whether you were in Las Vegas, Honolulu, Fresno, Cluj, or Seattle you always lived life to its fullest. Your successes have been mind-boggling and have transformed lives. Now, you face this challenge and once again you will conquer it because that is just who you are.

I love you and am so proud of you!

Love,
MaryAnn

Scott says he'll keep praying too!

Finally, in May of 1998, I received the following letter:

May 8, 1998
Dear Dr. Baird:

Congratulations! We are pleased to inform you that you have received a passing score on the Psychology Written Examination administered on April 8, 1998. We have enclosed the cumulative data from that examination for your review. The passing score for this examination was a raw score of 140 or 70 percent.

Your Score: 141 or 70.5 percent

When I finally passed, I felt more relieved than anything else. I think I was happier for those people around me than for myself. I thank God for this blessing and try to use this difficult experience to make me a better psychologist and person. Even though, Lord, I could have learned a lot without taking so many exams. A recap of that journey is as follows:

Date	Score (Percentage Correct)
4/94	64 percent
10/94	66 percent
4/95	68.5 percent
10/95	68 percent
10/96	68.5 percent
4/97	65.5 percent
10/97	69.5 percent
4/98	70.5 percent

To put my licensing exam attempt number eight in perspective, if I had gotten just two more answers wrong out of those two hundred questions, I would have failed again. Whew!

With that adventure behind me, I registered to take the state oral exam. I was confident that this exam would be easier to get through. I would have to make an oral case presentation about one of my clients, in front of three psychologists, demonstrating my knowledge of state laws pertaining to psychologists and psychological ethics. At the time, I was doing crisis intervention work for Compass Health. For my case presentation, I prepared one of my outreaches to one of the homes I had visited where a client was in crisis. I spent several months getting ready for the orals, which were the final step to becoming a psychologist.

On January 8, 1999, I took the oral exam and felt pretty good afterward, confident that I had passed. Three weeks later, the letter from the Department of Health came. When I opened the letter, I was nervous, but I was certain that I had made it. The letter started out: "We regret to inform you that you did not pass the oral examination." *Oh, no, not again!* I was in shock! At first, I thought they had made a mistake. I called the next day to verify that it was really me and that there had not been some type of mix-up. No mix-up, it was me. It was hard to believe. No stats were involved, just straight clinical work and the law. I later received feedback that I needed to present a case about a client whom I had been seeing on an ongoing basis, not a one-time crisis intervention. I would have to wait one year before I could take the exam again. So down on my knees again, asking the Lord, *What now? I don't have any ongoing clients!* I didn't want to quit my job on the Children's Crisis team, but I couldn't use any of those cases for my orals presentation. The Lord answered my prayer quickly.

A few days after receiving the bad news, I was talking with my supervisor at Compass Health and he suggested that I call someone at Catholic Community Services (CCS) who was in charge of the outpatient program for children. It was a great connection. For the next year, I volunteered my services at CCS and saw clients—children, teens, and families—on a weekly basis. I enjoyed being at CCS and prepared a good case for the upcoming oral examination.

I waited my year and took my second re-examination. I was again confident after my oral case presentation, but I had also been confident the first time. When the letter came in the mail a few weeks later, I was looking for just one word at the start of the letter. It was there, in bold print: **Congratulations!** Thank God! Mission finally accomplished, with a lot of persistence from me (I guess I just don't know when to throw in the towel), much support from many, and God's abundant grace.

Through the years, I am always still learning, but no more tests, and no statistics! Being a licensed psychologist, you are required to attend twenty hours a year in continuing education to keep your license current, so I attend several seminars a year based on my interests in the field. These seminars are excellent: I can just sit back and take in all the information, with no worry about an exam at the end.

What I learned from my school experiences was that if you don't have good study habits earlier on, you'll pay the price later. Good study habits mean not just putting in the time, but knowing how to study the smart way. Previously, I tried to memorize everything but didn't fully understand the concepts, especially in math and statistics. My good friend Jan Flom gave me some good tips and walked me through how to write a basic essay. I was learning these skills from her after I had already graduated from UNLV and was doing undergrad work in psychology at the University of Hawaii.

I also learned that it's never too late to follow the path God has for you. Prayer and reflection can really help you try to stay on that road. I wouldn't give up on myself until God did. I'm confident to say, if I hadn't passed that damned written state exam, I would probably still be taking it today for the __th time. Because I know God never gives up on us.

FAMILY

"Dear friends, since God so loved us, we also ought to love one another"
(1 John 4:11).

If you had asked me while I was growing up who my hero was, I would have named Floyd Patterson, boxing champion. If you asked me now, I would say my dad. Let me explain by what I said at his memorial rosary on May 17, 2003.

It is finished. The words Jesus said right before He went up to Heaven. As you know, to gain eternal life you must first leave your earthly home. Knowing my dad, the following probably happened, right after he died. Suddenly, he would be standing in line at heaven's gate to be judged. His mind would be racing. "Now let me see, there has been some grey areas in my life, maybe I've cut some corners, walked close to the line, but I've been a good husband and father. I've given back to society in many ways. Gosh, the line is getting shorter. Now let's see. I need to calculate the pluses and minuses of my life. This should be a quick process because I have it here all in my head." When he reaches the front of the line, Dad would begin to say to St. Peter: "I have it all figured out, now here's a list of all my assets and liabilities. As you can see, the assets list is longer than the liability list. Now I know I was the one who did the books but . . ."

At that point, St. Peter would stop Dad and say, "Jack, Jack, it's okay. You don't have to add everything up. I already know all about you. Come on in."

At that moment, Dad would be a little shocked and probably be thinking, "Boy, that was easy. If it would have been me, I would have checked those books a lot closer. St. Peter would have never worked for me, but this is great: I'm in!" After sizing up Heaven and seeing Mom, family members, and friends again, Dad would go looking for the head man, the general manager of Heaven, so to speak. After finding Him, he would put his arm around the Lord and say, "It's a great place you have here, Lord, I really like it, but could you please show me where your suites are?"

Looking back on what I said over ten years ago, I would have added more of the human side of Dad. Yes, he was a great business-man. Yes, he had a wonderful attention to detail. And yes, whenever we traveled as a family we stayed in suites, but there was more to him.

I have the chance now to write about the other sides of Dad Baird. He knew all his employees' names and about their families. He stopped to talk to everyone; from the janitor to a VIP guest, he treated them all the same. He expected everyone to do their job well, but it was more like a team approach. He groomed his hotel managers in a fatherly way and had their overall interests at heart.

You could tell that he really loved my mother and would do any-thing for her. He grew up learning that money equals security. Thus, through the years, he obtained quite a bit of wealth. He wanted my mother and us children to be taken care of, if something happened to him. My dad paid off our home in a very short period of time because he didn't want the mortgage hanging over his family's head if he died. He was a hard worker and invested his money wisely. When my father died, he had money set aside for my sister and me that blessed each of us. My father equated money with love. If you really loved someone, there would be a financial safety net for them if needed. At the same time, we were expected to find our niche in the world and get paid for it. My sister and I both accomplished that.

On the suggestion of my wise mother, my dad took my sister to Europe when she was in the 5th grade. My mom had noticed that my dad really didn't know Mary Ann well and that at times she appeared timid of him. I guess it was easier for my dad to talk to me about sports and other guy things. A lot of fathers wouldn't have taken that advice and would instead deny that there was a problem. Some dads might have agreed and then spent more time with their daughter around the house or taken her out for an occasional ice cream. A few might have taken their daughter out of town for a weekend. Not Dad Baird. He took my ten-year-old sister to Paris! They really got to know each other, and it really helped to grow and deepen their relationship when they got home. What a brilliant suggestion by my mother and loving follow-through by my dad!

Growing up, I used to spend hours in my dad's study, listening to his stories of business and management. My dad was always interested in what I was doing and asked me a lot of questions. It was embarrassing to be with him in public at those times when he would brag to strangers about his two kids. At the same time, we really felt he was proud of us.

My dad really got to know my friends. I remember one time, my best friend, Ted "Newy" Newman, came to pick something up from my house when I wasn't home. He had left his car running in the driveway and ran to the front door for a quick pick up. He was greeted by my dad and the two of them began talking. They went to Dad's study, just for a few minutes, which extended to the point that when Newy came out to leave, his car had run out of gas! My dad had a special way of keeping you interested because you always felt that you were a part of the conversation.

Dad was a master planner. Take a look at his meticulous schedule of the 1960 Christmas party for all the relatives. This was a big gathering at the Bairds' home, especially on my mother's (Eisen) side.

7th Annual Eisen Holiday Party
3:00   Arrival time
3:45   Children's movies (Cartoons, Western, Our Gang Comedy)

4:45	Children's and young adults' buffet (fifteen years and under)
5:30	Santa comes (Give out Grandma's gifts . . .)
6:30	Adults' buffet
	Children's movies (Mighty Mouse, Three Stooges, W. C. Fields)
7:30	Carols (all sing)
7:40	Bingo (five games, one grand prize) (World's Fair four-feet poodle)
8:25	Movie time for all (*The Night before Christmas*; *The Nativity*)
9:00	Free time
9:05	Departure

After that particular holiday bash, my parents decided to celebrate Christmas out of town from then on. I never knew the real reason, but spending next Christmas at Disneyland, I really didn't care. We spent wonderful times together as a family without the distractions we would have had at home during Christmas. Through the years, our Christmases moved from Disneyland to Hawaii and ended at Palm Springs: great memories during those special times. Even though we were in beautiful places, most of my thoughts are with the people I shared them with.

My dad was my hero. He even called me on his own, after my mom had died, to sing "Happy Birthday" to me each year. When I won the election at UNLV for treasurer, he ordered a cake with gold coins on it to congratulate me. Yes, he was quite a man, who sent us to Catholic school and was with us at mass with Mom on Sundays. Dad liked to stand in the back. He believed in God and had a special relationship with him. My dad lived by faith through his actions and by how he treated his fellow man.

My mom was the unsung hero of the family. She did so much behind the scenes for all of us, never asking for any applause. She was my hero. Mom spoke the loudest with her letters, art, and poems, and through her gentle but firm guidance. Most important of all for me was her unconditional love. So many times Mom was there to give me support and love during disappointing times.

An example of this was a letter she wrote when I had just found out I had failed the state's written psychology exam again.

> February 3, 1999
> Dearest Jeff,
>
> My heart aches for you. Failing the exam this time was devastating, really devastating. You could not have been prepared, when you thought you had done well. I wanted to reach out and give you a big hug. Consider it's on its way. I felt your pain—mothers do that.
>
> You have a tremendous abundance of ability and you rebound from the most difficult situations, where the majority of people are defeated— you arise and get help to find solutions.
>
> You will survive. You will attain your goal and ultimately you will get your license. The time schedule for this is as always in God's hands.
>
> We are so proud of you. Nothing changes that and you never cease to amaze us when you are faced with another obstacle that seems insurmountable—you manage to overcome it.
>
> As always your cheering section is ready to shout and cheer! Plus, we are ready with any type of help as needed.
>
> We love you so much our hearts overflow, number one son.
>
> Much love,
> Mom

I always felt that I was the most important person in the world with my mom. She was a great listener and a wise lady, who knew when to give advice and when to let me figure it out. Her love for all of us was apparent on a daily basis. A handmade card she made for my dad on their wedding anniversary really showed that love.

> Dear Jackie Bear,
> We've been married for forty-seven years.
> There has been great joy, much laughter and some tears.
> There was always your love, constant and true,
> And my love for you grew and grew.
> Our life together has been a wonderful journey,
> With more to share from here and into eternity.
> All my love always,
> Patsy Ann

Her character is revealed in excerpts from several letters she wrote to her younger brother, John, from 1996 to 1999, on important subjects:

Feelings—My first choice is sharing my feelings by writing. So, John, we share a common way of communicating and I think it is a good thing. Those who receive word from us have the luxury of being able to read what we have written as many times as they want. The spoken word is powerful but it is never quite as tangible.

Art—I watched painting classes on PBS which ranged from watercolors to acrylics to ink. The techniques each artist exhibits is fascinating. I've learned a great deal about mixing colors, and I can now look at paintings I did years ago and realize how they could have been done better if I had the knowledge I have now. So, John, please find the time for your art, even if it is a little time. I even think God might think it is a good idea. I'm sorry for being such a nag, it's just that I care.

Pain—I'm not sure how long I can keep this up. Trust me, I will never give up easily, they will have to come and take me away. Often, I make a joke concerning my illness, when you have chronic pain, humor is your best friend. Some of our jokes might seem odd but it works, it really works.

Religion—The scope of what we learned in Catholic school was dreadfully limited. The attitude of those teaching us in a simplistic format. I remember finding that situation unacceptable when I was in college. I wanted answers to my questions in an adult level. I know heaven is a wonderful place, and I will be very happy to see those loved ones who are there already, especially our two babies we were never able to hold.

Behind that beautiful smile was a smart lady. You probably have heard the saying: "Behind every good man there is a good woman." This doesn't hold true in the case of my mother. With her, it should be: "Behind every good man is a great lady."

Dad talked over all major business deals with my mom before he went forward. Dad was very hesitant before investing with other business associates about buying the Kennedy Hotel in downtown Seattle. After my mom heard the whole story, she replied, "You should go into the deal only if you're the managing partner, because then we know it will be a success." She was right, and the hotel was.

Mom was the glue that kept the family together. She was the calming voice that settled things down. Mom wasn't quick to react. She thought it over, then let you know her point of view.

I got my sense of service from my parents, especially my mom. She was involved with numerous charitable organizations all her life. From Children's Hospital to the lady down the street, my mom was always there when there was a need. She did this in a quiet way, never trying to bring attention to herself.

Her faith was lived the same way. My mom usually mentioned God in her letters to me or over the phone when she was giving me support. At her memorial rosary, Mom just wanted a poem to be read. As you read it, you'll see and feel her concern about others, not herself. I was deeply blessed to have a mom like her.

Dear Family and Friends,
How am I feeling? What are my thoughts?
Please read this special poem and think of me:

"I'm Free"
Don't grieve for me, for now I'm free.
I am following the path God laid for me.
I took God's hand when I heard the call;
I turned my back and left it all.

I could not stay another day.
To laugh, to love, to work or play.
Tasks left undone must stay that way,
I found that place at the close of the day.

If my parting has left a void,
Then fill it with remembered joy.
A friendship shared, a laugh, a kiss.
Ah yes, these things I too, will miss.

Be not burdened with times of sorrow,
I wish you the sunshine of tomorrow.
My life's been full, I savored much,
Good friends, good times, a loved one's touch.

Perhaps my time seemed all too brief;
Don't lengthen it now with undue grief.
Lift up your heart and share with me.
God wanted me now, God set me free.
—Author Unknown

All my love,
Patsy Ann Baird

On January 13, 1991, I landed in Romania to work a year with
World Vision. Also on January 13, my future wife Monica was born.
I believed that God sent me to Romania to work with the orphaned
kids. He also had other plans. I met Monica at the orphanage in
Cluj, three weeks after I arrived. She had just started working there,
too, as a translator for Medicins Sans Frontieres (MSF)—Doctors

Without Borders. I remember meeting her at my first meeting with MSF and World Vision. She wore a green skirt that matched her beautiful green eyes. Monica had a free spirit about her and really appeared to enjoy life to the fullest. We began dating in February and we married on December 7 that same year. I knew pretty soon in the dating process that Monica was the one for me. Two events really sealed the deal.

The first one happened a few months into our relationship. We had an argument about something, which of course I can't remember now. It was on a Friday, and we had plans for the weekend. We were at her apartment and in an angry huff, I told her, "I'm leaving." I stormed out of the apartment. I later learned that Monica's mother told her to go after me but she didn't. Most women I had dated in the past would ran after me. After I got a few blocks away from the apartment building, I felt I had to make a decision. *Do I keep going home and be without her the whole weekend, or do I go back with my tail between my legs?* I went back.

The second event was a month before I proposed to her. We were walking back from a party we had attended. It was early in the morning and the streets were deserted. I asked her hypothetically, "If you were to get married, would you like to have children?" The answer was "Yes."

"If you had children and your husband wanted them to be raised Catholic, would that be all right?" The answer was also "Yes!" Not too subtle a line of questioning, but I got the answers I was hoping for.

All right, then, if she would accept, I guess I am getting married. After thirty-eight years, I had found, I mean God led me to, the right woman.

We were married on December 7, 1991. It was a glorious wedding, which started at the courthouse. The mayor of Cluj did the honors. Cristi was my best man and also did the interpreting. When it came to "Do you take this woman to be your wife?" Cristi told me to say "Da," which meant "Yes," but I said, "Sigur ča da," which meant "I sure do!" This broke up the crowd into laughter and even put a smile on the serious mayor's face. We walked to the gothic-style church in the middle of town on a snow-covered day. All of Monica's friends and family were there. The staff of World Vision from all over the country came to share in this wonderful moment. My family was pleased and excited about the wedding but couldn't make it. Being married in the church, in my eyes, would make the marriage official. The Mass was glorious, with a choir singing and two priests presiding over the service. You could feel the presence of God blessing Monica and me. Then we were off to the reception at a hotel overlooking Cluj, where the dancing, eating, and drinking went on for hours, in true Romanian style. It was joyful to see everyone having a great time and celebrating our marriage.

Best of all, I had married the girl of my dreams. I must say, it was a very good day! Later that month, we had a chance to visit my parents, my sister, and her family in Palm Springs, California, for Christmas. World Vision paid for our airfare. It was great to show off my beautiful bride. Then we went back to Romania for a year.

When we arrived back to Seattle to live a year later, my parents had a one-bedroom apartment all set up for us to move into. They furnished it with various pieces of furniture they had. All we had to do was start paying the mortgage. It was very remarkable and humbling to realize all the work they had put in to have a nice place ready for us to stay.

There was a cultural adjustment for Monica, living in the United States. At times it was hard, even with our many blessings. I remember the first time she went into the produce section of the grocery store. When Monica saw all the fruits and vegetables, she cried. It brought back memories of growing up in Romania, where nothing was in abundance. If by some chance some fruits came their way, a long line would await you.

When it was time for Ted to go to school, fitting in with the other school moms was another challenge. Many of the mothers already knew each other. With being new to the country and having an accent, she felt a little on the outside looking in. But being the tough cookie that she is (but very sweet, I might add), Monica adapted and made things work. She has been hosting a school mom get-together at our home for over ten years, even though all the children in Ted's class are now away at school. Monica has many friends from Ted's days in school but she had to earn it by never giving up.

Monica felt it would be important for Ted to be raised in an environment with other children, so she opened up a daycare in our home. From early in the morning until the evening, she cared for up to six kids at one time. For the love of our son, she did this exhausting job. Through the years Monica has been a gift from God with her love, support, and wisdom. Married twenty-five years at the time of this writing, I can't imagine being in a world without her.

Ted Patrick Baird was born February 7, 1994. Being a father for the first time, I didn't know what to expect. The birth of our son left me in awe and almost without words; he was truly "a miracle from God." What a joy to be a father and have our family!

With my job at Compass Health as a children's crisis worker, I could be home a lot during the day and night when it was slow at work. It was a great opportunity to watch Ted grow. He was a happy guy but also had his own opinions. By the age of five, Ted had his own ideas on how he would like to be dressed. When it was time to buy clothes for him, he wanted to go to the store with his mom to pick out his own fashion styles. He went to Holy Rosary elementary school and Archbishop Murphy high school. Basketball was his sport, although he also played soccer, baseball, and ran track. He was a talented basketball player, playing AAU during the off-season and high school ball during the season. I am proud to say that he made the junior varsity (JV) team when he was only a freshman. When the season opened his junior year, he started on varsity.

During his sophomore year of high school, he started his own urban wear line called Classiq. Ted's line consisted of hoodies, T-shirts, and tank tops. He did it all, from setting the right prices to working with the screen printers to the marketing and shipping. Everyone loved his clothing design, and it was very exciting to see other people wearing Classiq. Ted has spent hundreds of hours learning the business and gaining interest for his brand. Ted picked the University of San Francisco (USF), a Jesuit school, as his college. Ted spent two years there, learning business and getting a feel of campus life. He joined a business fraternity and settled in. He transferred to

Academy of Art University-San Francisco to focus on design and the hands-on part of the fashion business. Ted graduated on May 11, 2017. Monica, his grandmother and myself attended the wonderful ceremony. When he took us on a tour, his school was impressive. The rooms were not like your typical classrooms. They were large working areas, where the students can create and get hands on experience that can translate to the real world. His mother and I couldn't be prouder of the fine young man he has turned out to be. Ted is the master of getting me great birthday and Father's Day cards. In his last card to me, he had the following letter enclosed:

Dad,

Happy Belated Birthday! Please excuse the tardiness of this letter. In no way does its tardiness represent my love and appreciation. This presents me with a tall task. To write a card well enough to make up for the severe lateness. You never ask for anything and I know how much these cards mean so I wanted to collect my thoughts so I could express my thoughts and feelings as clearly as possible. I was thinking where I could start this letter off and one incident stuck out immediately.

If my memory serves me right, I came home one day from Holy Rosary. It had to be in the 7th or 8th grade. I was writing a paper or had a project on someone who inspired me and I said Martin Luther King Jr. was my hero. You were taken aback from my answer (rightfully so). At the time I had little to no idea why you were sad but after growing as an individual my vision has become 20/20.

The moment a man becomes a father his priorities completely change. The focus is centered around providing the best possible life for that child. You have sacrificed so much for me and have done so in upmost humbleness. That is one of the many attributes I try and embody from you. Your incredible kindness to friends and charity amazes me because you do so not for the recognition, but for the sake of helping others. "What type of man are you when no one is looking?" With all this sacrifice, I can't even begin to thank you. Although it took me some maturity to fully realize all the opportunities you have given me (go to private school, start clothing line, travel, live in SF, attend art school and so much more). With that maturity I have come to another conclusion, that Martin Luther King Jr. isn't my hero. You are my *hero*. You embody all the qualities I look at in an ideal man. Assertive humbleness with an unparalleled ability to empathize with anyone. Thank you for being a role model who leads by actions and not by empty words. Every day I try and embody you and I hope to be the same man with the same moral discipline. Thank you again for everything you have done and continue to do. It never goes unnoticed. I'm blessed to call you my dad. With much love,

Ted

Even though Ted usually remembers his parents on important dates, he did forget once on his mother's birthday. To make up for it, he flew in from San Francisco without her knowing. When Monica came home from work, there was a huge, beautifully wrapped box in the middle of the living room. When she got close, Ted popped out like a jack-in-the-box with flowers in hand. Monica let out a shout and was initially in shock and leaned backward into me (I was behind her, just in case), and then a big smile came out. The four days Ted was in town, he just hung out with his mom. We all forget things and have setbacks. The true character of a person is what they do next. Very proud of my son!

Mary Ann Parker, my sister, five years younger than I, is truly a blessing to me and to everyone who is around her. She and her husband, Scott, live in Virginia. They have two great children, Jackie and Sam. Jackie has a master's degree in social work and is working with the chronically mentally ill in Maryland. Sam, after getting his bachelor's degree in religious studies, moved to Seattle with some friends. He is working in the business sector, at Copper work distillery, while deciding whether he wants to return to school to get a master's degree or go to law school. Scott, while being a super golfer, is also a bright and successful businessman in the technology field. I will always be thankful to Scott for showing me how to make a super batch of popcorn. Mary Ann has been an attorney for AARP for over twenty years. Her job involves trying to help seniors stay in their nursing homes. Her big heart and skills as a lawyer have helped countless seniors through the years. My sister has a feisty nature at times, especially for injustices against her clients. You should think twice about going into battle against her! It's great having her in your corner. Mary Ann jumps in with both feet as a wife, mom, professional, friend, and sister.

One time at the pool, she was watching her young child take a group swimming lesson. Suddenly she noticed that the instructor wasn't paying attention and her kiddo was under the water and not coming up! Mary Ann jumped into the pool with all her clothes on. Now that is jumping in with both feet! She is very inspiring and I'm so blessed to have her as a sister.

Monica's brother, Stefan, married a wonderful lady, Marcela, and they have two wonderful adult children, Stefania and Oli. In 1989, Stefan swam the Danube River pulling four friends on a raft to freedom from Communist Romania. Marcela and the girls later joined him in Canada. Marcela worked her way up from being a maid to executive housekeeper at the Westin Wall Center, Richmond, British Columbia. Stefania got married to Anil in 2016, and they live in Vancouver, Canada. Stefania has a master degree and is doing great work as a reference librarian for the law firm of Larson and Lundell. Anil is a passionate and creative High School Art Teacher for almost twenty years. They visit us throughout the year, and it's always a joy to have this bright and inspiring couple visit us. Oli, creative talented and independent young woman, moved to Bristol, England, a few years ago and is enjoying her time there.

Monica's mother, who is eighty-eight at the time of this writing, lives in her own apartment close by us and spends a lot of time with her daughter. Momo, as I call her, is full of life, and it is a joy to be around her. Her English is getting better and better. Momo is a super cook and prepares Hungarian dishes, which are delicious. Monica's father, whom I asked for Monica's hand in Romania, died several years ago. He did have the chance to visit us in the United States after Ted's birth. He was always full of energy with a big laugh. He even played Santa Claus at Christmas at the orphanage.

Last but not least are my friends. My best friend, Ted "Newy" Newman, has been a source of inspiration and support. He can always make you laugh. Newy has been my running partner on several of the races. My other great friend is Willie Jack, whom I met at Shoreline Community College. We were both on the track team. Willie has been a super friend for over forty years. Jan "Janner" Flom has been another dear friend from college days. We worked at the state mental hospital in Honolulu together. We also suffered together, me more than she, when we took a stats class at the University of Hawaii. Janner was one of the driving forces behind me getting through undergrad studies in psychology. She taught me the fine art of studying.

There have been other good people who have passed my way, but no one can compare to my three amigos Newy, Willie, and Janner!

What have I learned from my family and friends? Their love and faith in God. Through good times, uncertainty and sadness, they were always there. Laughter and trying not to take things so seriously is another blessing I have learned along the way. As the years go by, the memories become more important to me: The Christmas trips with my parents and Mary Ann, which grew to include her family and Monica and Teddy. The destinations we visited were exciting to see, but to me, the deepest memories are from the people whom I shared these vacations.

We as a human race have our share of problems. Because of that, I wonder why we can't be more understanding. As the late Dr. Dale Turner, *Seattle Times* religious columnist, wrote: "Be kind. Everyone you know is carrying a heavy burden."

BEFORE YOUR BABY COMES TO BREAST OR TO VISIT YOU WHILE IN THE HOSPITAL
PLEASE DO THE FOLLOWING THINGS TO PROTECT YOUR BABY AND OTHERS.

. Wash your hands with rubbing alcohol.
. Do not unwrap your baby while on your bed. The nurse who brings your baby in the
first day will unwrap and show you that your baby is all right. After that please
co-operate. The Baby's linen has been sterilized to prevent infections of all
types and if the baby is unwrapped while on your bed the linen is no longer sterile.
. Do not put your baby under the covers with you for the same reasons as above.
. Relatives or friends are not allowed to remain in the room when the baby comes in
. Visitors to see baby in groups instead of singly to avoid disturbing the baby.
6. Not to sit on occupied or empty beds. New patients expect a clean bed.
7. Children under 14 years of age are not permitted to visit on this floor at any time.
8. If you would like formula to take home with you, please bring a sterile bottle with
you.

Baby's name and sex. Boy Paul
Room Number. +78
Birth date. 4-29-53
Time of birth. 10:03 am
Birth weight. 9#
Length of baby. 9 0 1/2
head 14 1/4
Chest 13 1/4

Ready or not, here I come

Little Jeff's 2nd Christmas, 1954

Dad reading from the bible to Mary Ann and me, Christmas 1965

Mom and Dad, the early days, 1956

Mom and Dad, Palm Springs, 1996

Dad's 76th Birthday with Monica, July 13th 2000

A pick-me-up drawing from my Mom

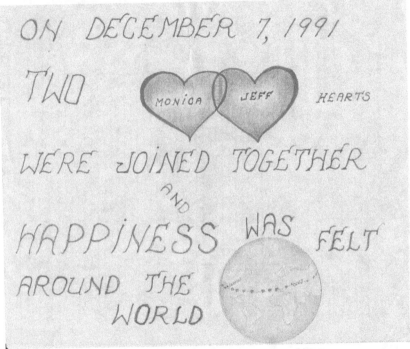

ON DECEMBER 7, 1991

TWO MONICA JEFF HEARTS

WERE JOINED TOGETHER

HAPPINESS AND WAS FELT

AROUND THE WORLD

One of my Mom's wonderful drawings

Dear Family and Friends,

How am I feeling? What are my thoughts? Please read this special poem and think of me:

I'M FREE

Don't grieve for me, for now I'm free.
I am following the path God laid for me.
I took God's hand when I heard the call;
I turned my back and left it all.

I could not stay another day.
To laugh, to love, to work or play.
Tasks left undone must stay that way,
I found that place at the close of the day.

If my parting has left a void,
Then fill it with remembered joy.
A friendship shared, a laugh, a kiss.
Ah yes, these things I too, will miss.

Be not burdened with times of sorrow,
I wish you the sunshine of tomorrow.
My life's been full, I savored much,
Good friends, good times, a loved one's touch.

Perhaps my time seemed all too brief;
Don't lengthen it now with undue grief.
Lift up your heart and share with me.
God wanted me now, God set me free.

Author Unknown

All of my love,

Patsy Ann Baird

October 20, 1999, Mom (74) went to heaven,
poem was handed out at her rosary

Another friend has passed away
I hardly even knew
My name for him was "Happy Jack"
For he made us happy too

He decorated just for us
His hallway was a treat
Looked forward to his change of theme
Every season, it looked neat!

At Christmas time 'twas Santa Clause
On Halloween black cats
Then in the spring came Valentines
Then Easter eggs perhaps

He never missed a single chance
To hand out chocolate treats
We Thank you Jack for the pleasures
They were yummy and sooo sweet

We are thankful, having known you
Having shared your life so short
We shall keep you in our memories
"Happy Jack" a "Happy Sport"

To Happy Jack from his unhappy family

From Elaine Smith

May 8,th 2003, Dad (78) went to heaven, this note was put on his door.

Presidential Ball, January 1989, Goerge Bush Sr.
Sister Mary Ann, me, Susan (Newy's future wife) and Newy (Left to right)

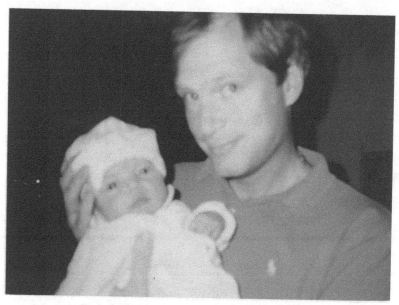

Proud Dad with Teddy, February 7th 1994

Monica and I going to the Holy Rosery Roaring
Twenties Themed Auction, 2006

Ted driving the lane

Stefi and Anil's wedding, August 6th, 2016.
Me, grandmother Olga, Niece Oli, Mother of the Bride Marcela,
Stefi, Anil, Aunt Monica, Cousin Ted (Left to right)

Ted's Graduation, Academy of Art University, San Francisco,
May 11th 2017. With his mother and grandmother in the background.

The Parker Family in Palm Springs, Mary Ann
and Sam, Scott and Jackie, 1996

Jackie and Sam at the Great Wall of China
wearing Ted's *Classiq Brand*, 2017

Willie's 50th Birthday

BOXING

"We are pressed on every side by troubles, but we are not crushed.
We are perplexed, but not driven to despair.
We are hunted down, but never abandoned by God.
We get knocked down, but we are not destroyed"
(2 Cor. 4:8–9).

I was introduced to boxing at a young age. At around eight years of age, my father wanted me to experience the manly art of self-defense. I didn't want to be a man at this point, and I remember crying all the way to the gym. My first sparring encounter was with a boy around my age. It was a disaster! I got hit all over the ring. I was learning how to become a punching bag, not a boxer. Dad and I kept coming back each Saturday. I still wasn't into it but I was learning some skills, like not getting hit in the head all the time. Four weeks later, I had to fight the same kid who really gave me a pounding. It was a different story this time, with me doing the hitting and him doing the catching. I really felt a sense of accomplishment in overcoming a fear I had.

My dad knew what he was doing and I had learned a valuable lesson. Defeat, hardship will come, but if you increase your skills in that area and keep trying, amazing things can happen. I won both my boxing contests at the age of eight, then retired.

I had two more fights when I was sixteen because my friend Mike Shanks began training at the Wallingford Boys Club. Knowing how to throw a punch, block a punch, and move around the ring was important. Even more important than that was endurance. To go full out for three two-minute rounds doesn't sound like a lot of time but it is an eternity, waiting for that bell to ring.

My first fight was with a boy of the same shape and size. The only difference was that I was looking good in my black and orange robe and boxing trunks. I looked like a boxer; he looked like a farm boy with his cutoff shorts and didn't even have a robe. While the referee was going over the instructions at the center of the ring, I was thinking, *This will be a short fight. This guy definitely doesn't know how to fight.* The bell rang, and I came out swinging, basically throwing everything I had learned in the gym out the window. I found out quickly: *This farm boy can hit like a mule.* He knocked me down in the first round. I got right up but really didn't know where I was. In the corner after the first round, I didn't know if I really got knocked down or even what round it was. I battled back for the next two rounds and I was told it was a close fight. My opponent won on a unanimous decision.

We went to lunch after the weigh-in of my next and last boxing contest two weeks later. When we found out we didn't have to fight each other that night, we were both very happy. He went on to win his next fight by stopping the kid in the second round. My opponent, I remember seeing him knock the stuffing out of the guy he fought last. When the bell for round one rang, he came rushing at me; maybe he thought I looked like a farm boy. I got out of the way. I noticed he had a big tattoo on his arm and hair on his chest. *Wow, a grown man!* I got on my bicycle and stayed away from his flying fists. Out of desperation I even got some punches in, which only made him angrier. At one point, he mumbled through his mouthpiece, "Slow down, you bastard." *Oh no, now he's swearing at me, he must be really mad.* I lasted till about the end of the third round. I ran out of gas, even used up the fumes. I couldn't even raise my arms, I was so tired. The referee stopped the fight. I wasn't hurt like the last match, but I can't remember having ever been that spent. The only thing close would be the last few miles in a marathon. I retired again from boxing at the age of sixteen.

The boy, I mean man, who beat me went on to become a professional fighter. He had an unremarkable career except for one fight. He was one of five boxers who fought George Foreman in one night. He was knocked out by George, but he fought a champion. So my claim to fame in boxing is that I was in the ring with a guy who was knocked out by George Foreman, Heavyweight Champion of the World. I don't think that will get me into the Boxing Hall of Fame, but it is cool to think that I fought a guy who fought a heavyweight champion.

When I was ten years old, my dad took me to my first boxing match. It was Heavyweight Champion Sonny Liston vs. Floyd Patterson. The previous year, Liston knocked out Patterson in the first round to take his title away. Floyd Patterson was my favorite fighter and I thought he could beat Liston this time. That prediction was wrong and he was knocked out again in the first round. I saw the fight live in a Seattle movie theater. The big fights were shown all around the nation live in theaters or auditoriums, which they called Closed Circuit. It was exciting to be with my dad with mostly men in the audience. There were only a few kids there, so I felt special being with my dad watching the fight on a school night.

Going to fights with my dad and my actual boxing experience started my love for boxing. I even recited a poem by Cassius Clay (Muhammad Ali) in sixth grade and came in second place. I remember the poem went something like this: "This is the story of Cassius Clay, the most talked about fighter in the world today/this kid has a left, this kid has a right/and when he hits you once you're asleep for the night/and while you're on the floor while the ref counts ten, you'll pray not to fight him again."

The '60s, '70s, and '80s were all great decades for professional boxing. Muhammad Ali, Smokin' Joe Frazier, Larry Holmes, George Foreman, Sugar Ray Leonard, Roberto Duran, Marvin Hagler, and Thomas "Hit Man" Hearns. I saw all the major fights, first with my dad, then riding the bus with friends to see them on Closed Circuit. I had the chance to see Joe Frazier fight live in London in 1972 and Muhammad Ali defend his heavyweight title against Ron Lyle in 1975 while I was going to school at UNLV.

My favorite fighter was Floyd Patterson. I liked how he fought in the ring with his quickness and fast hands. At the age of twenty-one, he was the youngest boxer to win the Heavyweight Championship. Floyd later became the first ever to lose and regain the title. Even with those accomplishments, he will never be in the circle of the greatest Heavyweight Champions. I'm fine with that because of the kind of man he was; I really looked up to him. Floyd was a humble, gentle, and faith-filled man in a brutal business. He once knocked his opponent through the ropes and then helped him back into the ring. Once he knocked the mouthpiece out of his opponent's mouth and when it hit the canvas, Floyd went over and picked it up to give back to the fighter.

In the world of fighting, he had a sensitive side that knew great emotional pain. Like most fighters in his era, Floyd Patterson came from the bottom rungs of American society, looking to boxing to achieve a better way of life. He was at Wiltwyck, a New York school for emotionally disturbed children. Floyd's book about his life story, *Victory over Myself*, published in 1962, really gave me insight on the man behind the gloves. A man of few words, who would rather be by himself than in a crowd, was the fighter I really looked up to. He didn't toot his own horn but showed what he was made of in the ring and outside the ring. In the 1960s he was involved with the civil rights movement. Floyd traveled to Birmingham, Alabama, in 1963 to show support for Dr. Martin Luther King Jr. What Floyd said at the end of his career really summed up why I liked him so much. "I have been knocked down more than any other heavyweight champ in history," Floyd says. "But it means that I've also gotten up more than any other heavyweight champ in history. I'm proud of that" (Berkow, 1986).

In 1981, my best friend, Newy, came back to Honolulu to put on "So You Think You're Tough" boxing shows. When I heard of the idea, I replied, "I love you, buddy, but you're crazy." Newy followed a similar format in Washington, of tough-man contests, which had been very popular. Ads were put in the newspaper and flyers were put up in bars, gyms, and other places where we thought tough guys hung out.

Newy hired professional trainers to have the wannabe fighters come to their gyms and work out for the upcoming show. They would make the matches up by weight and experience. This would be the first professional fight for all the participants. Newy really had a flair for showmanship and the local sports media really ate it up with a lot of newsprint. He was interviewed several times for the evening sports segment of the local news. I was working full-time at Annabelle's, thus being behind-the-scenes guy. I handled the money, organized the staff who would work the shows, and suggested any ideas I had. Thus I was the silent partner, which was fine with me. Newy had the style, energy, and fearlessness that made him a great boxing promoter.

The first "So You Think You're Tough" show had 2,300 fans at the Blaisdell Arena on March 24, 1981. The Blaisdell Arena is Honolulu's main showcase for major events and seats around eight thousand. Andy Yamaguchi of the *Honolulu Advertiser* newspaper wrote that the first "Toughman" card was one of the year's few local boxing shows to finish in the black. Winners of the fights win $100, losers take home $50. Miller Beer paid for the local paper advertising, and we had $1 beers at the fights. The second Tough-Man boxing match was at the Blaisdell Arena on May 12 with around two thousand customers. Getting more than two thousand fight fans to a boxing contest is really an accomplishment on the islands. Past boxing promoters had presented seasoned professional fighters with known names in the sport and drew in the low one thousands. We learned that boxing shows had a low presale of tickets as most fans will come on the night of the fight to buy their seats. For both Blaisdell Arena shows we had under one thousand tickets sold presale.

I remember on the night of the first fight, a fight Newy told anyone who would listen would be a huge success, we were at Blaisdell, looking out onto the large empty parking lot an hour before the fight. What happened next reminded me of the movie, *Field of Dreams*. The movie's main character was told, *"If you build it, they will come."* At the end of the movie, you could see the headlights of cars coming to his empty baseball field in the middle of farmland. We could also begin to see the fans coming to the fight and the parking lot filling up.

It was exciting and rewarding to know that total strangers were willing to pay their hard-earned money to come to a show you helped create. They came, and by the cheers we heard, they had a good time. Headlines of the sports pages declared: "Tough Guys Have Themselves a Ball," "That's Entertainment," "Rocky Sequel a Winner," and "The Crowd Gets Into 'Tough' Boxing."

The third and last promotion was at the Hilton Hawaiian Village on July 16, 1981. Under the chandeliers, the show had a paying crowd of 1,063 and a gross gate of about $6,300. For this show, we didn't have to pay for the venue where the event was being held. We could use the Hilton's ballroom for no charge. We would make our money on ticket sales and Hilton would make their money on drinks and food. "It was a night of friends bringing flower leis to their fighters and a lot of 'Aloha' in the building. It was also a night where we had our first women fight," F. Lewis, a sportswriter from the *Honolulu Advertiser*, wrote.

On a night when Bloody Marys outnumbered bloody Rockys, and more olives went down than fighters, boxing went ballroom in Hawaii.

Never before has the victim of a punch been able to look up from his landing place and see a pink chandelier. But then, never before have paying customers watched from behind white cloth-covered tables while ordering drinks, either.

What it was boxing's version of "That's Entertainment" at the Hilton Hawaiian Village's Coral Ballroom last night.

"It was interesting . . . entertaining, but I don't think I'd call it boxing," said Bobby Lee, the Hawaii State Boxing Commission's leading purist.

Indeed, if there was an air of boxing to be found in Knock Out Promotions "So You Think You're Tough" card, it was in the air as smoking was finally allowed at a boxing event for the first time since Blaisdell Center prohibited it five years ago.

It was a night of friends bringing flower leis into the ring for the winners—and losers: a night where one of the participants almost missed his bout because he couldn't find the dressing room and where several fans almost wound up at the Jim Nabors Show by mistake.

The gimmick is to allow some with boxing potential and others with only Walter Mitty dreams to act out their fantasies in the ring for modest renumeration ($100 for the winner, $50 for the loser).

The curious came primarily to see Trudy Andres of Ewa Beach win a unanimous decision over Debra Lavatai of Honolulu in a three-round welterweight bout in which neither's flesh nor pride were injured. It was a decidedly better fight than the historic but inept first women's bout here five years ago.

I learned a lot from my boxing experiences. Boxing was a connection for me; boxing was about relationships. It was a sport that my dad had me participate in as a boy. At first I didn't like it, but by not giving up, I overcame my fear of trying something new. As a boy with my dad, with mostly other men in attendance, I saw professional fighting for the first time. I felt important being with my dad. I learned from the boys I fought that after three rounds of trying to take another guy's head off, there was a mutual respect with no hard feelings after the fight. It was a great experience to be with my buddy Newy, putting on the Tough-Man contests. I really learned from him, to not just talk about an idea you have, but to put it into practice. He came over the ocean to fulfill a dream to put on boxing shows that would make money.

From Heavyweight Champion Floyd Patterson, I learned the lesson that when you get knocked down, you get back up. He was the first heavyweight champ to lose the title, then win it back. In life, as in the ring, it's important to keep your chin down and keep moving forward. If you get knocked down, get back up. With the grace of God and support of family and friends, this can be done.

Slugger Baird, Second row from right

With Floyd Patterson after his knockout of Charlie Harris in 1971

Newy and I with our homemade boxing poster

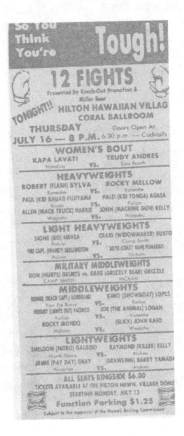

Pat (Da Sting) Ching VS Sheldon (Nitro)
Gadigo Blaisdell, May 12th 1981

Kapa vs Trudy
Under the chandeliers at Hilton Harrison Village

RUNNING

*"I have fought the good fight, I have finished
the race, I have kept the faith"*
(2 Tim. 4:7).

From an early age, I always knew I was fast. Pick-up football, games of chase and keep-away on the playground, I was faster than most everyone else. In seventh grade, I finished first in the 75-yard dash at the Catholic Youth Organization (CYO) Championships. I ran track in eighth and ninth grade at Nathan Eckstein. With Gerald Singletary anchoring the relay team, we were almost unbeatable. Gerald would later receive a full track scholarship at the University of Washington.

My next three years of track were at Bishop Blanchet High School. In the district meet, I ran the third leg of the 880-yard relay. When I got the baton, we were five yards behind. I ran like my life depended on it and I got us a slight lead. We knew with a lead, our anchorman Dave "Fu" Funsen could bring us home victorious. He held off Gerald Singletary from Garfield High School to win the race and punch our tickets to State Meet, where we came in sixth. My senior year, I anchored Blanchet's mile relay team and we came in second at State. Our track coach was Ed Thenell, a bear of a man with a gentle soul. He died at 36 years old. For being on this earth for such a short period of time, Coach sure left his mark on the hearts of many.

After Blanchet, I went to Shoreline Community College for two years. I joined Fu on the team there. We were a ragtag bunch of guys, turning out just for the love of the sport. There wasn't any pressure on keeping your scholarship (there weren't any) or preparing for any big meets (there weren't any). It was a lot of fun to compete for just the sake of the sport. I also met a lifelong friend, Willie Jack, who threw the javelin. I didn't run in the second year because I wanted to keep three years of eligibility left when I went to a four-year school.

My grades were good enough to get into the University of Nevada at Las Vegas (UNLV). I walked on the track team. Most everyone had a scholarship. Some were from the local high school, others were out of state, and a handful of athletes were from different countries in Africa. From the onset, the two races I ran at Blanchet and Shoreline, the 100- and 200-yard dashes, weren't going to cut it. I could hang with my fellow university-level sprinters in practice, but they had an extra gear that I didn't have. I moved to the 440-yard dash (once around the track) and it was a good fit. You had to be fast to compete, but you also needed endurance. The runner needed to be strong when he hit the 330-yard mark and, as we say, "the bear jumps on your back." I knew that God gave me the ability to run, and with hard work and dedication in my training, I could increase my endurance and beat some runners who were naturally faster than me.

My first semester at UNLV and on the track team was fun. Meeting a lot of different people from all walks of life was great. As always, I gave 100 percent in practice and tried to push my abilities to the limit. I remember one afternoon almost at the end of the first semester, I was walking back to the frat house from morning classes when I ran into the head coach, Gordon Edwards. He asked me to come over to speak with him. I thought, *I must be in trouble for something.* Coach Edwards said, "Bairdo, I have some good news and some bad news for you. The bad news is it's going to be a really hard work out today and it's going to be really hot." After he told me that, I was thinking, *Well, duh. It's Monday, and after practice we usually crawl back to the locker room. So no big surprise.* Coach then said, "The good news is you're on scholarship." I later found out that our pole vaulter had gone back to California, leaving one scholarship open. I was in shock and floated the rest of the way home. The scholarship paid for my out-of-state tuition and books. It was more than simply a savings of money for my parents but also felt like a validation of my hard work and faith. I was so proud when I told my parents about the scholarship! It also meant I was good enough to compete with other Division One athletes.

I ran the three years left of my eligibility for UNLV. I ran the 440 with a personal best of 49.5; 220, 22.2; and 100, 9.9. I ran on the 440, 880, and mile relay. I was track captain during my senior year at UNLV. We traveled in white station wagons throughout the western states. Ours was a modern-day wagon train with four to five vehicles lined up. My three years of running track were a great experience. I really liked and admired our head coach Al McDaniels, who took over in my junior year when Coach Edwards left. His wife, Cheryl, became a big part of the team and a second mom to a lot of us. Coach Al was an experienced track athlete who was very successful in his day. He was firm but funny in a tell-it-like-it-is type of way. Two stories about Coach Al will shed some light on a man you can't help but love.

My first year, we had an indoor meet in Arizona. I won my race, but Coach felt I would have gotten a better time if I had been up against better competition. So the next year, he put me in one of the featured races of the day, the 500-yard dash. I found out before the race that there would only be three of us running. I was told after the race that the other two runners were both Olympians. The indoor track was smaller than the outdoor track, thus the turns were sharper, which makes it interesting for a 6'3" runner like me. As it turns out, the track could have been straight as an arrow, it wouldn't have mattered. I ran right with them for two-thirds of the race, then they started to pull away and got farther and farther ahead of me. All the time, Coach Al was right there on the side of the track, screaming, "Looking good, Bairdo, keep your form." At the start of the last lap, I was way behind, but Coach was right there in front of everybody, yelling, "Keep going and you'll break the school record." I was thinking that the only school record I was going to break was having the fastest time getting off the track and into the locker room. Coach Al was in front of hundreds of spectators, cheering me on. If I would have been him, I'd probably have gone somewhere under the bleachers to hide. I was off the school record by a few tenths of a second.

The other story happened at an outdoor meet at Loyola Marymount in California. One of our sprinters was injured so we had to do double duty. I was in four relay races, three where I had to run 440 yards and one 220. I was used to running two 440s in a meet, but never three. I psyched myself out and didn't run any of them very well. After the meet, we paraded into the gas station with our band of station wagons to fill up. Coach Al was in the driver's seat of the lead wagon when he called me over. While walking over to him, I was thinking *He'll probably say he is sorry for overloading me up today. He might also say I gave a good effort and next week will be better.* When I got to his car, he looked me in the eyes and said, "Bairdo, you sure were crappy today." I smiled weakly and walked away, stunned. After a few minutes, I laughed to myself and thought, *Coach was right.* I never had another track meet like that again. Coach Al really cared for his athletes and with his wife, Cheryl, really made it a family affair. He always told it like it was.

Throughout the years, I kept active, running a few miles a week. It was enjoyable just to take off from my front door, music playing, running a few laps around the neighborhood. At the age of fifty-one, for some unknown reason I got it into my head that I wanted to run a marathon. I first wanted to run the 26.2-mile race with my son, who was nine years old at the time. I didn't realize how grueling a feat it would be or that it had a minimum age requirement of eighteen years old. I was disappointed because I thought this would be something fun to do with Ted. I later found out that fun wouldn't be the best word to describe a marathon. Monica saved the day by volunteering to run a half-marathon while I ran the full marathon.

Even though I ran a few miles a week throughout my life, I felt we needed someone with long-distance knowledge to help us. We joined Team In Training, the world's largest endurance sports training program. The trainers had great knowledge and passion for running. We were given a training log, which was filled out for exactly what we were supposed to do. For our long runs, we ran as a group in various locations on Saturdays. We all raised money for the Leukemia and Lymphoma Society. It took over five months of training and was a lot of fun, especially because it was something Monica and I could do together. It's amazing what you can accomplish if you start out slow and steady with the encouragement of others.

The marathon was in Phoenix, Arizona in January of 2005. My best friend Newy flew in to run the marathon with me. Monica was primed for her 13.1-mile race. It was a hot day, but Newy and I felt great halfway through the race. We were laughing and really feeling the pump of the adrenalin. We started to slow down around mile 15 and at mile 18 I hit the wall (a term meaning "you're toast," "running on fumes," or "the wheels fell off your wagon"). I completely slowed down to a run/walk shuffle. Newy appeared to be in better shape, so I told him to run on even though we had agreed before the race, we would finish together. After some persuading, Newy agreed to run ahead. I was in bad shape but I was going to make it one way or another. Newy told me later that he was feeling bad about leaving me, so he came back. The rest of the way, with my best friend at my side, I ran, walked, limped, and waddled to the finish line. Our time was five hours and two minutes, which I was told was good for a first-timer. When Monica first saw me after the race, she was in shock. My lips were blue and I was as white as a ghost. She, on the other hand, was looking good and full of energy after the half-marathon run. There was a dinner and dance set up later in the evening and amazing but true, we all danced.

I didn't know it at the time, but I had acquired the runner's bug. Shortly after running my first marathon, I was thinking about the next one. Even though I was sore and physically and mentally it was one of the hardest things I ever did, I wanted more. I remember Monica and Newy had a "We'll see" attitude about the next race. I had some minor injuries that slowed me down for the rest of 2005, but I did get the chance to run the Kirkland half-marathon and the Las Vegas Marathon. The Kirkland race was memorable for all the hills and having my fastest half-marathon to date, one hour and fifty-five minutes. The Las Vegas Marathon was exciting because I was back where I went to school. The marathon was held early in the morning and it was pitch dark. We started at the beginning of the Las Vegas Strip, and with all the bright lights, it was spectacular. There I was with a field of 10,951, heading up the Las Vegas Boulevard. During the race I saw a group of running Elvises: they all had the full Elvis look except for running shoes. There was a group of couples who got married during the race. They were dressed up in wedding attire except for shorts and running shoes. Along the course they popped into one of Vegas's famous in-and-out wedding chapels and away they went as man and wife.

The greatest sight that topped them all was when I was a few miles into the marathon and away from the lights and crowd. On the side, on a vacant sidewalk, stood my UNLV track coach, Al McDaniels. He was cheering me on again like he did thirty years ago! I ran over and gave him a hug. That was a very meaningful experience for me. I guess once a coach, always a coach. Monica and Teddy were rooting me on at the finish line. Monica even had tears in her eyes as I slowly walked over to her after I finished.

In 2006, I ran the Anchorage Marathon and had my best time to date, four hours and fifty-nine minutes. Before the start, an official was telling us what to do if we encountered a bear. It was a beautiful race in the hills and forest area of Anchorage without a bear to be found. Also that year, I ran the Disneyland Inaugural Half-Marathon. You run through the two parks, Disneyland and California Adventure, at the beginning of the race. It was fun seeing Mickey Mouse, Donald Duck, and the rest of the gang cheering you on.

In 2007, I ran the Paris Marathon with Monica and 42,195 of our closest friends. We started at the back of the crowd of runners. You could see the Arc de Triomphe right in front of us. I asked Monica several times before the race if she had to go to the bathroom. It is important to take care of your needs way before the race because the lines get very long at the porta-potties. The gun went off and the runners slowly moved forward. After a few minutes, we were getting closer to the starting line, when Monica told me she had to go to the bathroom. *Oh no, not now,* I thought. I asked if she could wait. No, she couldn't. In line she went as I was pacing back and forth, getting more nervous by the second. Some of the people in line at the porta-potties weren't even runners. When Monica was done, we began sprinting to the starting line because all 40,000 runners had already gone. The marathon staff was deflating the huge start arch and as we reached it, they lifted it up so we could get under it and be officially timed on the mat that activates the timing chip you wear on your shoe.

There wasn't another runner in sight as we started out, and I was anxious because I didn't want to take the wrong winding street and get lost. Then a remarkable event happened. Because we were in last place of the thousands of runners, it was like being in the lead, but in reverse! We became the only runners on the street and they began calling our names, which were printed on our racing bibs, as we ran by. We felt like elite runners for a brief period of time before we got up to the rest of the runners. It was the hottest Paris Marathon ever run, around eighty degrees. They ran out of water at several of the stations along the course. The firefighters were hosing people down if you wanted a blast of cold water. The French do things a little differently: at mile 22, they were handing out cups of wine with cheese. We made it through the 26.2 miles with Monica having more energy at the end than her coach, me. Ted broke from the crowd and ran a short distance with us near the finish line, which was pretty cool.

In October of 2007, I ran the Portland Marathon, a popular race in Oregon that had 7,800 runners that year. I dedicated this race to Andrew Walsh, who died on June 24, 2007 from a brain aneurysm at the age of thirteen years old. He was a classmate of my son at Holy Rosary School. His motto was "Never, never, never give up." Andrew, his parents Rob and Kyle, have been an inspiration to me and my whole family. I had his name on my running bib and spectators from the crowd were calling out to Andrew. I looked up to heaven and said, "They're cheering for you, kid."

My sixth and final marathon was in 2011 at the Marine Corps Marathon. This race was run for my dad, who was a marine who served in the Korea War. This was the thirty-sixth running of the event, which is held in Washington DC. A turnout of 20,895 runners started this historical race. My sister, Mary Ann, and brother-in-law, Scott, who live nearby in Virginia, were on hand to cheer me on. They even had a big sign that read, "Go Jeffo!" Thanks, Parkers!

To date, I have run twenty-four races, which includes six marathons and eighteen half-marathons. The training is less intense for the half-marathon and the recovery time is much faster. I have been fortunate to run several half-marathons with my Phoenix warrior running buddy, Newy. He once wore a shirt during a race that said on the back, "In Dog Years I Would Be Dead." As you can imagine, he got quite a few comments during the race.

Another way of getting enjoyment out of running is training someone. I had the pleasure of training my niece Jackie for a marathon. I sent her a personalized running log for the five months she needed to get ready for the race. Jackie followed it with great determination and has finished the Baltimore and Washington DC marathons. After the second marathon, she sent me a package to thank me for training her. By the size of it, I thought she sent me a T-shirt from the DC marathon. To my shock, when I opened it up, she had sent me her hard-earned finisher's medal. Jackie also sent me a beautiful card.

> Dear Uncle Moose,
> Hope all is well! When I received my medal after the race I knew immediately I wanted to give it to you. I would have never finished two marathons without your guidance and support. Running has become such an important part of my life and helped me in so many ways. I know my medal will be in good hands. Also, I know you need to have at least one running medal since you said you have given the rest away. Love, Jackie

The medal Jackie gave me is the most important one of the twenty-four ones I received by running the race myself.

I have been running all my life. In that time, I have found an aspect of running I don't like at all: injuries. I have gathered a team of professionals who have kept me on the road for the most part. This awesome group is anchored by Dr. Mark Reeves, Podiatric Sports Medicine at Virginia Mason. I always come in with a multitude of questions, and he answers them all, even at times with what I don't want to hear. I have limped into Mark's office several times and I'm surprised when he tells me I can't run. The hardest thing about not being able to walk is not being able to run. My physical therapist is Dr. Jeff Waldron, who is really invested in getting you healed. Jeff will get on the floor with you, take you outside, and watch you run. He even went to where I work out (Super Fit) to see what exercises I should eliminate for the time being. Super Fit trains you in strength and conditioning in a group format. Throughout the years working out there, my core strength has greatly improved. The owner, Jeff Turner, trainers Linda Lee and Eddie Barruga, are right there putting you through the paces. Their encouragement, knowledge, and even humor help you get stronger without hurting yourself. Mary Margaret, massage therapist, has done an excellent job getting my legs loose and keeping on the road. Mary Margaret's motto is "When you need me, I knead you." She is a woman of faith, so when she is getting the knots out of me, she gives witness on how God has blessed her life.

What I have learned from my running experience is that it's another way to give glory to God. Running fast as a youth helped me in many areas growing up. It helped me to get into Blanchet High School, earn a scholarship at UNLV, and overall increase my confidence. I tried to use my God-given talents to the best of my ability. It's quite a feeling when you're running down the track and no one can keep up with you. I hope I've learned along the way to be thankful for the blessings you have. My speedy days have long passed. I run longer distances now at a slower pace. This has been a spiritual, emotional, and physical experience. When running on the Burke-Gilman Trail or around Green Lake, there are times when you are in the zone and it is heaven on earth. The spiritual, emotional, and physical all come together and it's pure joy. Running has been a great outlet for me my whole life, and I thank God for it.

I thought the previous paragraph was going to be the ending of this chapter. My editor asked me to expand it and make some life connections. At the time I couldn't think of anything to add, so I didn't give it much thought until a week later. I came up with some ideas to add to the chapter. Guess what I was doing when the inspiration hit me? You're right, I was running.

I have mentioned before that I have always run throughout my life. It serves many purposes. Using the example of running a marathon, you can make similarities with life in general. Before running a longer distance, you have to start with shorter distances and gradually increase your mileage. You learn how to train for a marathon by listening to experienced runners and reading all you can. You also listen to what your body is telling you. Being consistent with your training is a key to success. Just as in life, it's wise to have goals and a plan on how to achieve them. It's wise to listen and learn from others but also to look deep inside one's soul.

During the first part of the marathon, you're with thousands of runners; you have trained hard for this and you're feeling that you could run forever. Like in life, having a great day when things are going well, you walk around with a smile on your face.

Around the thirteen-mile mark, halfway through the race, you start to feel some fatigue and aches and pains. Around the twenty-mile mark, with six miles to go, you're in a considerable amount of pain. Your body wants you to stop; your hair even hurts (that might be a slight exaggeration, but I guess you get the point). That's where your mind takes over and tells your body: "We're going to do this." In life, there are times when you could be in emotional and physical pain. There are unexpected challenges that come up. Running, especially at times when it is difficult, helps me practice to run through the anxiety and worry in life, not around them. Using my mind, body, and soul to help me attain a goal, not just in running but in life. You're trying to give glory to God during the wonderful times and during the tough times too. In running, as in life, you need to keep your head up, keep going, and trust in God to take you where you are supposed to be.

High School State Track Championship, kissing my medal, 1971

UNLV Track team, 1974

Coach Al's retirement party

Marathon De Paris with Monica, 2007

Marine Corps Marathon, 2011

Finishing a half-marathon with Newy in Bellingham, 2012

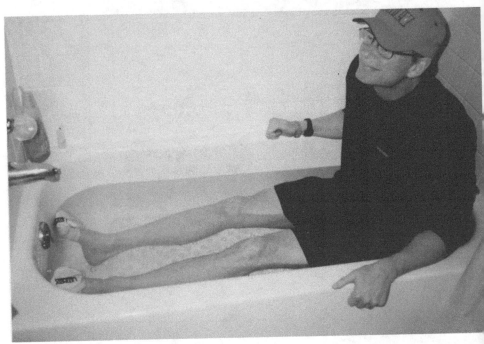

Ice bath after a long run, it keeps me on the road.

DISCERNMENT AND HOPE

"The discerning heart seeks knowledge"
(Prov. 15:14).

Looking over my life, I can see that I have definitely taken some wrong turns along the way. With the grace of God, I have learned from them. I'm very sorry to those whom I have hurt. Usually my pride or hurt feelings has gotten in the way.

Some of my most important decisions in life have come through discernment and the help of others. The way I understand discernment is to know God's will. What does God want me to do in my life? To free up the channels of communication, I must not be centered on myself and my needs but be centered on our Lord. "Be still, and know that I am God!" (Ps. 46:10).

From *The Little Book of Mother Teresa*, the following prayer speaks of how silence begins a wonderful journey.

> The fruit of silence is prayer.
> The fruit of prayer is faith.
> The fruit of faith is love.
> The fruit of love is service.
> The fruit of service is peace.

I need a quiet place to reflect and pray: One place is at our church, Holy Rosary. Most every Friday night, Monica and I go to Holy Rosary. We're usually the only ones there. As Catholics we call it Adoration, spending one hour with our Lord. Where to go next and how to proceed are questions I bring before God. No, I don't receive a lightning bolt from heaven with my answers. If I'm still and being open, I do receive a direction in my total being. As I mentioned earlier, this is how I made my decision to go to Romania. Going back to school to study psychology was placed in my heart by God. Finding the right woman to marry, opening up Affordable Counseling, the list goes on.

To let God in, I need a quiet place and a quiet mind. In Henri Nouwen's book *Discernment,* he wrote the following: "To want to know God's plan and purpose without regular prayer and engagement with scripture and God's people is like trying to bake a cake without assembling the various ingredients. Discernment grows out of the life of faith rooted in community." Throughout my life, even at a young age, I was encouraged by my parents to say my prayers at night. Growing up in my family, going to Catholic school, the celebration of the Mass and faith were discussed. My mother talked freely about her faith and it showed in how she treated others. During my time in Hawaii I was a lector at Mass. Worshiping in community is a very powerful experience for me. Young and old, eyes to the altar of the Lord, giving thanks and praise for his glory.

Another way of discernment is meeting with a small group of men every other Sunday for the last fifteen years. The group is called SacraMentors and was founded by Lory Misel and Father Bob Camuso. The following format is followed during each meeting:

1. Be still and open yourself to the Lord.
2. Share your mistakes, problems, fears, and pain.
3. Experiences of love and appreciation you have encountered.
4. The things you studied.
5. Acts of service.
6. Be still and prayer offering.

Each brother has a turn to share each of the above parts, while the other brothers listen without comment. My group of holy men: Mark, Allen, Bob, Angel, and James, have been vital in helping me to do God's will.

Each day is a blessing and a struggle at times, especially when I try to live it my way. By saying the daily Rosary, Bible readings, and reflection in the morning and spiritual reading in the evening, it helps keep me on the right path even when I fall down and just think of myself.

Father Nouwen's book also describes discernment as revealing new priorities, directions, and gifts from God. He wrote, "We come to realize that what previously seemed so important for our lives, loses its power over us."

Especially during Lent on a daily basis, I practice another form of discernment. St. Ignatius introduced *The Examen*, which builds on the insight that it's easier to see God in retrospect rather than in the moment. Father James Martin, in his book, *The Jesuit Guide to Almost Everything*, has slightly modified *The Examen*, which I find easier to follow.

1. Gratitude: Recall anything from the day for which you are especially grateful and give thanks.
2. Review: Recall the events of the day, from start to finish, noticing where you felt God's presence and where you accepted or turned away from any invitations to grow in love.
3. Sorrow: Recall any actions for which you are sorry.
4. Forgiveness: Ask God's forgiveness. Decide whether you want to reconcile with anyone you have hurt.
5. Grace: Ask God for the grace you need for the next day and an ability to see God's presence more clearly.

Without discernment in my daily life, when the big decisions come along, I could just be swept away by my emotions. I'm not saying this doesn't happen, when my pride gets in the way. I find that if I'm doing my daily spiritual devotions, I can get back on track sooner and let our Lord lead. This sense of peace of being where I'm supposed to be in life is very satisfying. J. Oswald Chambers wrote that "peace is not the absence of trouble but the presence of God." I see a direct connection with peace and discernment, also with hope, which I will write about next.

Hope has been an important part of my life. To live in the now, hope for the future. For me, hope creates action in the present. Hope is a central theme in many religions.

Throughout history, hope has helped people get through difficult times. From Viktor Frankl's 1959 book, *Man's Search for Meaning*, which has more than twelve million copies in print worldwide, hope and faith saved lives. Between 1942 and 1945, Dr. Frankl labored in four different concentration camps, including Auschwitz, while his parents, brother, and pregnant wife perished. Dr. Frankl reported that the loss of hope can have a deadly effect.

The prisoner who had lost faith in the future—his future—was doomed. With his loss of belief in the future, he has also lost his spiritual hold; he let himself decline and became subject to mental and physical decay. Usually this happened quite suddenly, in the form of a crisis, the symptoms of which were familiar to the experienced camp inmate. Usually it began with the prisoner refusing one morning to get dressed and wash or go out to the parade grounds. No blows had any effect. He just lay there, hardly moving. If this crisis was brought about by an illness, he refused to be taken to the sickbay or to do anything to help himself. He simply gave up (Frankl, 1959).

Most of my clients whom I see in counseling have lost hope in one or several areas of their life. As my own dissertation showed, hopelessness is a major factor of depression and having suicidal thoughts. What I have tried to do through the years is to give my clients a sense of hope when they leave our first session together.

In Bernie Siegel's book *Peace, Love, and Healing*, the power of hope is illustrated in the following story:

In the *Journal of the American Medical Association* (henceforth referred to as *JAMA*), a physician writing pseudonymously as Jane A. McAdams told about how a message of hope affected her mother at a time when doctors were expecting her to live only a few weeks more. Her mother had grown up during the Depression and was as a consequence very frugal and opposed to waste of any kind.

"I resolved to lift her spirits by buying her the handsomest and most expensive matching nightgown and robe I could find. If I could not hope to cure her disease, at least I could make her feel like the prettiest woman in the entire hospital.

"For a long time after she unwrapped her present . . . my mother said nothing. Finally, she spoke. 'Would you mind,' she said, pointing to the wrapping and gown spread across the bed, 'returning it to the store? I don't really want it.' Then she picked up the newspaper and turned it to the last page. 'This is what I really want, if you could get that,' she said. What she pointed to was a display advertisement of expensive designer summer purses.

"My reaction was one of disbelief. Why would my mother, so careful about extravagances, want an expensive summer purse in January, one that she could not possibly use until June? She would not even live until spring, let alone summer. Almost immediately, I was ashamed and appalled at my clumsiness, ignorance, insensitivity, call it what you will. With a shock, I realized she was finally asking me how long she would live. She was, in fact, asking me if I thought she would live even six months. And she was telling me that if I showed I believed she would live until then, then she would do it. She would not let that expensive purse go unused. That day, I returned the gown and robe and bought the summer purse.

"That was many years ago. The purse is worn out and long gone, as are at least half a dozen others. And next week my mother flies to California to celebrate her eighty-third birthday. My gift to her? The most expensive designer purse I could find. She'll use it well" (Siegel, 1989).

In the Bible there are several references about hope. One of my favorite passages is from Isaiah 40:31: ". . . But those who hope in the

Lord will renew their strength. They will soar on wings like eagles; they will run and not grow weary, they will walk and not be faint."

A person of discernment is a person of hope. With our God, family, and friends, we always have hope. Hope always! I wish you all God's very best!!

WORKS CITED

Berkow, Ira. (1986). *Red: A biography of Red Smith.* New York, NY: Times Books.

Duchane, Sangeet. (2004). *The little book of Mother Teresa.* New York, NY: Fall River Press.

Frankl, Viktor E. (1959). *Man's search for meaning.* Boston, MA: Beacon Press.

Martin, James. (2010). *The Jesuit guide to (almost) everything: A spirituality for real life.* New York, NY: HarperOne.

Nouwen, Henri J. M. (2013). *Discernment: Reading the signs of daily life.* New York, NY: HarperOne.

Siegel, Bernie S. (1989). *Peace, love & healing.* New York, NY: HarperCollins.

ABOUT THE AUTHOR

Jeff Baird is a psychologist and founder of Affordable Counseling. He also serves the counseling needs at his parish, Holy Rosary. First time author, long time story teller. Jeff lives with his lovely wife Monica in Edmonds, Washington, and they have an amazing son Ted who lives in San Francisco.

CPSIA information can be obtained
at www.ICGtesting.com
Printed in the USA
FFHW01n1907131018
48760200-52855FF

9 781641 405836